EARNING PASSIVE INCOME THROUGH RENTAL PROPERTIES

Invest in Real Estate and Live off Your Rents. How to Do it With No Money and No Previous Knowledge in Rental Property and House Flipping

Table of Contents

Introduction 5
Chapter 1 - Understanding Rental Property Investment 9
   Why Rental Property? 9
   Two Ways to Earn Profits with Rental Property 12
   Developing the Right Mindset for Rental Property Success 15
Chapter 2—Great Location, Great Investment 20
   Classes of Real Estate, Where You Should Invest. 20
   Four Important Factors for Evaluating a Neighborhood. 22
   How to Spot an Emerging Real Estate Market. 24
Chapter 3—Choosing the Best Property 27
   Residential Real Estate to Invest In 27
   Types of Commercial Real Estate 29
   The 1% Rule for Investing in Real Estate 32
   Essential Questions to Keep in Mind When Evaluating Property 33
Chapter 4—Financing Your Rental Property 37
   House Hacking: Make Money and Live for Free 37
   Creative Ways to Finance Your Rental Properties 39
   Start Saving for a Down Payment Right Now 41
Chapter 5—Real Estate Tools for Success 47
   Strategies for Building a Successful Rental Property Portfolio. ... 47
   Commercial Real Estate, Another Means to Build Your Portfolio
.... 50
   10 People You'll Need on Your Real Estate Dream Team 53

Chapter 6—The Rental to Outshine All Others 55

    10 Steps for Rehabbing Your Rental Property 55

    The Most Important Rehabs for All Rental Properties 59

    Home Improvements to Instantly Boost the Value of Your Property 61

Chapter 7—Managing Your Rental 64

    Finding Great Tenants for Your Rental 64

    Strategies for Managing Rental Property 70

    12 Must-Know Tips from Rental Property Experts 75

Chapter 8—Precautions 81

    Good reasons to let go of rental property. 87

    Five Crucial Exit Strategies for Your Real Estate Investments 89

Conclusion 92

Introduction

Does your uncle rent out his second apartment for $1500 a month and you want in on the action? Living the life of a landlord is a dream. Consider the possibilities: If you could rent 10 apartments for $1500 a month each, you could easily add $15,000 in passive income to your wallet every month for the rest of your life. Have you ever rented from a landlord who owns 5, 10 or maybe 50 condos, and makes a full-time living simply by renting properties? Do you ever wonder how they got there and got funding? In most cases, landlords didn't inherit their properties. They started out with a few acquisitions and expanded their ownership to numerous properties.

Do you want to get started in real estate but don't know where to find funding? There are ways to buy rental properties without being a millionaire. This book will teach you all the secrets you want to know about rental properties. If you have little or no money at all and don't know where to start, we'll teach you how to finance your rental properties without a significant investment. Yes, it's possible - and yes there are ways to secure hundreds of thousands of dollars without using your mom's house as collateral. We'll give you insight into the landlord mindset: You will learn how to finance properties with little to no initial investment and we'll tell you how to find tenants and enjoy a stress-free lifestyle for the rest of your life.

Revelation #1: Rental Properties Are Stable Income.

Renting is the easiest form of real estate investment, a lot easier than flipping properties full time. To become a landlord, you merely have to acquire a property and put it on the market. You'll be able to find tenants for even the worst, most run-down properties. Compare that to flipping, where the flipper has to put down a payment for a property, repair structural damage, refurbish the interior, and wait an average of six months while a house that might not sell at all sits on the market.

A landlord could technically purchase a property and rent it out the next day. So, you tell me which is easier, renting or flipping? The hard part of rental income is making a long-term profit. It's your job to learn how to finance multiple properties at once to be able to sustain mortgage payments from tenants and grow your portfolio. This allows you to create a mini real estate empire which you can use to lead a care-free lifestyle. However, getting there is the hard part. This book will teach you how to get your first rental properties.

Revelation #2: You Can Start With $0.

It's possible to start acquiring properties with $0 payment down or merely a few thousand dollars. Think you need to be a millionaire to become a landlord? Wrong! Rental income is far more risk-free than flipping income, as you could purchase the worst house and rent it out immediately – there's no need to repair the property. You don't have to spend money refurbishing the interior and you can get funding from private investors to purchase your rental property.

There are ways to convince financiers to finance your rental ventures in exchange for a monthly payment. Of course, the more money you have initially, the more money you'll get to keep in rental income at the end of each month. If you have a million dollars to spare, you could purchase multiple properties and start renting them out for serious income. If you have no money, you can reach out to private investors for funding or fund your properties via banking institutions. We'll show you the most viable methods to fund your rental properties for every budget.

Revelation #3: You Can Get Paid Every Week.

Tenants will deposit payments in your bank account every week or every month. Technically, you could purchase a property and rent it on a daily basis to tourists on AirBnb, if you're willing to deal with clients every day. Rental property has no restrictions on the type of tenants you're allowed to have. The safest rental scheme is to provide housing for the average American family that has 2.5 children and a dog. However, that doesn't restrict your income.

If you have a property in a central location with many amenities, you could charge three times the market average to rent to tourists. Depending on how much time you're willing to spend dealing with tenants, you can adjust your payment terms accordingly. If you are willing to deal with tenants every day, you could get paid by the day. If you want a stable check deposited in your account at the end of each month, you can rent out to families. The latter is safer, but less profitable. The only work you'll have to do is bi-monthly checkups and annual maintenance (property taxes, insurance payments, etc.).

Revelation #4: There Is Work Involved.

We won't lie to you - rental income requires a certain amount of work. You won't have to call in general contractors and stress on the property every day like a flipper, but you will have to do to the occasional repair. What if you get a call at 3 a.m. from a tenant who has a roof leak? You can't tell them "go fix it yourself". You have to hire a roofing contractor who can get the job done and deal with that contractor for possibly weeks at a time. You're legally obliged to repair the property or you could face legal prosecution with fines and possible jail time. If a tenant dies as a result of property maintenance, the burden is on you.

Each time a problem arises in one of your properties, you will get a call from the tenants and they'll expect you to show up and fix it. It's your duty to hire the contractors and ensure that living conditions in your properties are up to par with the standards imposed by your state.

Like with any other business proposition, it's possible to skip the menial work. If you wish to disappear off the map, you could hire a "manager" do all the maintenance work for you and sail off into the sunset. However, most landlords live right next to their properties and assist tenants as problems arise due to trust issues. The most dedicated landlords in cities like New York own thousands of apartments and they attend to tenant's needs personally.

Revelation #5: Things Can Get Personal.

Have you ever rented your own apartment when you were a young adult and struggled to make payments? People run into financial distress all the time and your tenants won't be an exception. Certain landlords refuse to get close to their tenants and keep a business relationship in case they have to evict. Things can get ugly when you're dealing with tenants. Don't forget you're dealing with humans with real lives. The father renting from you might not be able to make rent after he's been fired from his job and the decision to evict him and his family will weigh on your conscience.

You'll have to make hard decisions. What if you're dealing with a single mother who has two babies to raise and she just lost her job and can't make rent? She may not realize that you still have to make your mortgage payments. Will you fall behind them or will you forgive their mortgage payment? You'll have to decide if you'll let them stay or if you'll evict them and make a place for new tenants. Landlord life is not glorious in many situations, despite how it's portrayed on TV shows. The more lower income your housing units are, the more you'll run into people with financial difficulties.

We'll give you the landlord secrets straight from the devil's mouth: We'll teach you how to finance properties, how to find tenants, and how to make a passive income with minimal work. Let's go!

Chapter 1 - Understanding Rental Property Investment

Why Rental Property?

Joe has $150,000 to invest. Why should Joe focus on rental properties instead of flipping properties? Rental is a whole different ball game. Rental properties are for the long term. For one, Joe can purchase a property he rents out without modifying the interior of the house. He can also start making a guaranteed profit as opposed to flipping a house that has to stay on the market for six months on average. Rental properties are for people who want long-term money, and who want to reap huge profits from depreciation. How many boomers do you know who bought a house for $100,000 in the 80's which is now worth over $1,000,000? If you hold on to your property for a decade or two, the value is guaranteed to double. In the meantime, you can get guaranteed monthly payments from tenants. We will teach you how to purchase properties, attract tenants, and get them to pay off your mortgages. For now, we'll show you why you need to invest in rental:

1) Real estate appreciation.

House prices in America go up. If you buy in a mid-sized city with population growth such as Austin, Texas, you're bound to see huge returns in as little as a few years. Appreciation means the property will increase in value the longer you hold on to it. People were able to purchase houses for a lot less than they cost today. The average $250,000 suburban house with a picket fence went for $100,000 in the 90s. What's not to say that the average $250,000 house of today will not be going for $500,000 within 15 years? The growth is bound to happen - you'll either buy in now or you'll miss out in the long run.

Even if you ignore guaranteed monthly payments for each property, purchasing a property in a hot area means you'll make hundreds of thousands (if not even millions) over the long term. Remember, it's yours when you buy it (not the tenant's). You can sell and get rid of a property at any time.

The city and market have an effect on the appreciation. Historically, the wealthiest cities in the U.S., such as New York City and San Francisco, experience appreciation cycles and the average apartment in these cities can go for over $1M. However, you don't need to buy in Midtown Manhattan to get appreciation. You could buy in suburban Portland, Oregon and still see significant returns in 15 years. The best cities in which to invest are mid-sized cities with strong population growth. Do you know which cities have the highest growth per capita? They're not NYC or LA. They're mid-sized cities with booming economies such as Seattle, Atlanta, Austin, and Charlotte.

To be upfront, you will not make a significant amount of money within the first few years. You might not make any money at all within the first 5 years. However, you will double your investment within the first 10 years even if you invest in the most average neighborhood in the United States. Any decent area with good access to schools and convenience stores will do. You don't need exceptional and the property doesn't have to stand out. Go for a drive, and you'll notice almost all houses are average houses. Those houses increase in value as the U.S. economy produces more wealth. Get in on the action now or miss out.

2) Cash Payments from Tenants.

The tenant has to pay you by the month – you'll get a guaranteed $1000-2000 a month in profits for the average property. If you haven't figured it out, the average mortgage tends to be lower than $1000 while rents for a house are typically higher. This is where you'll make returns in the short term. If you don't have any money at all, you can make enough to cover a down payment on a mortgage and finance a $150,000 house. Once you become the owner, if your mortgage payment is $900 a month, you can rent the house for $1500 a month. This means your mortgage will be paid off and you'll have a few hundred left to spare. The tenant has to pay all bills unless and they're essentially paying off your mortgage. What's better than getting guaranteed payments without doing any work? You only have to pay the down payment, which is typically 20%. If that doesn't convince you to get into rental properties, nothing will.

If you have investment money to spare, you will keep all the profits without making mortgage payments. The $1500/month rent money will go directly in your pocket and you won't have to pay off the bankers – your only expenses will be the house insurance and yearly property tax, which is rarely above 2% of the total value of the property. Moreover, you have other rental avenues that are open to you. You could rent the property on a daily basis and charge a higher markup for holidays such as Christmas, New Year's, etc. This allows you to make two to three times the average profits of a rental property in your area. All properties rent out immediately, without any repairs necessary. House-flippers have to invest tens of thousands of dollars bringing a property up to current standards, while landlords only have to throw the property on the market.

3) Tax Rebates.

The IRS thinks rental properties are not the most profitable form of property and they have write-offs for virtually every type of property. Landlords can claim "losses" every year and get deductions for all their income taxes, which helps them keep more of their rental income. Rental investments are IRS-safe because the property appreciates and depreciates simultaneously. The IRS believes that properties depreciate due to tear and wear, however, the market is usually on the upswing and the property value for properties tends to increase.

The IRS gives landlords write-offs under a specific property depreciation system called "General Depreciation System" or GDS. The GDS states that an average property has a recovery period of 27.5 years, which the IRS deems to be the average useful life of a property. The IRS provides deductions of precisely 3.6% per year on each building you own. In effect, the property taxes will be lower than the write-offs you're allowed. Using a simple write-off, you can pay the property tax and keep more of your profits using the GDS write-off.

4) Inflation Works In Your Favor.

Inflation raises the value of the property, while your mortgage payments remain the same. If you obtain a fixed-rate loan, which is the most popular of loans, you won't spend a single cent more than what you agreed to initially. For example, if you pay $20K as a down payment on a $100K property and that property appreciates to $200K within 10 years, you'll still only owe $80K. In effect, you only paid $20K to acquire a $200K property over 10 years. Inflation is your friend over the long-term and the fixed-priced mortgage allows you to only pay what you originally agreed to, instead of the inflated price of the property after you acquired it.

Two Ways to Earn Profits with Rental Property

1) Long Term Rentals

The safest and most conventional way to rent is long-term: You rent to families or professional individuals who have a job and the ability to make monthly payments. This is a foolproof rental method that requires monthly engagement with the tenant, only when you're collecting rent. You don't have to show up every week and check up on them and you only have to meet them when it's time to collect the rent. Long-term rent is the way to go, because families sign 6-month or 12-month contracts which are extendable.

You can progressively increase the rent as properties in your area increase in value and the neighborhood becomes more desirable. For example, a house that rented out for $1000 this year might go for $1250 next year. Tenants don't like the rent increase? You'll find new ones in one week. The beauty of rental properties is that multiple people are competing for the property and you always have a viable pool of tenants to choose from, even in the most low-income areas. Here's how to calculate your bottom-line profits:

The 1% Rule of Long-Term Rentals

The 1% rule is the simplest calculation people use to estimate the profitability of a rental property. You can estimate the profitability of a rental property before you even purchase the actual property, which will give you an indicator as to how much bottom-line profits you'll have left with at the end of each month. The 1% rule states the following: If the GROSS monthly rent makes up 1% of the original purchase price, you should buy the property. If the monthly rent before expenses is less than 1% of the original purchase price, you should seek out other properties.

Let's say you find a house in decent shape for $100,000. How do you know if you'll make a profit renting it out? Simple: Use the 1% rule. The 1% rule states that your gross rent should exceed 1% of the original purchase price. The property has to rent out for at least $1000 a month if you want to make a Return on Investment (ROI). Under this rule-of-thumb, a $100,000 property has to rent out for $1000 a month and bring in 12% of the original purchase price in returns annually. In this particular example, the $100,000 property has to return $12,000 in annual gross profits before expenses such as property insurance, taxes, and bills. Your net revenue needs to be 6-8% of the total property value per year. This means that when you rent long-term, you should be making returns of $6000-8000 per year in pure profits on a $100,000 property.

The average net return of 6-8% per year is a great deal, but it's going to depend on the city and neighborhood. The nicer the neighborhood, the lower the rental returns. The flipside is that a 6% return on a $300,000 house is higher than a 15% return on a $100,000 house. The highest rental returns typically found in cheap run-down properties exist because the properties cost little to purchase and the rental price is still relatively high. In general, you should be getting a solid 6% return in nice neighborhoods with affluent tenants and 8-10% returns on low-income neighborhoods with riskier properties that are more crime-prone. Whichever one you decide, you should not settle for less than 6% in yearly net returns.

The Capitalization Rate

Landlords calculate the "cap" rate, which is short for the capitalization rate, of the initial investment. The cap rate formula is the following:

Yearly Net Profits / Home Value = Cap Rate

Example: $8000 / $100,000 = 0.08

In this case, 0.08 is the result we're getting or 8% net ROI in simple terms. The capitalization rate on a $100,000 property which makes a net turnover of $8000 per year totals out to 8%. Whether 8% is a satisfactory return for the amount of effort you put into maintaining the property is up to you to decide.

The same principle applies to properties with a much higher property value. For example, if you find nice properties which give you an 8% cap rate on a $500,000 investment, you could make significant cash flow which pays off the property and gives you a great living. On the flip side, an 8% cap rate might not be worth it in a high-crime area that takes a lot to maintain and has extremely high insurance payments. In theory, you wouldn't need to be wealthy to finance a down payment on a $500,000 house, but you would have to save up for a few years.

2) Short-Term Rentals

Short-term rentals are the opposite of long-term rentals: They're unstable and they require constant work. You'll have to deal with clients a lot more than you would with long-term rentals, possibly daily. When you deal with long-term tenants, you only have to sign a contract and check them once or twice a month when it's time for you to collect your check or carry out the odd repair. With short term tenants, you have to meet tenants every day and clean up after them to prepare the property for the next tenants. What's in it for you? The markup is significantly higher. If you rent a house to a family for $1000 a month that wouldn't require any work on your end, but you'd only be left with $1000 at the end of each month. However, if you rent the same house for $100 a day to clients on AirBnb, you could make $3000 each month, but then you'd have to work and maintain the property every day.

Short-term rentals are the way to go if you have the time and patience to deal with clients on a daily basis. This is an excellent opportunity for young property owners or established property owners who enjoy meeting people and socializing. What's better than offering value to society and making huge returns in the process? You're not restricted to short-term rent from websites such as Craigslist and AirBnb. Once you own the property, you can convert it to a mini hotel or a hostel. It's possible to place four bunk beds in each room and convert the property to a hostel, then charge each one of the tenants $20 a night to stay there. This can generate a lot more cash flow than renting the property to a four-person family. Short-term rental requires a lot more work than long-term rental, but the profit margins are significantly higher.

Developing the Right Mindset for Rental Property Success

The one thing all landlords agree with is that they're in it for the profit. However, individual motives for obtaining profit may be different. Some people become landlords to retire and live out the rest of their lives in peace. Some people become landlords to escape their 9-5 job and be able to survive without slaving at a dead-end job. Entrepreneurs who are motivated to become wealthy typically purchase multiple properties and rent them out while waiting for a high-ticket payout. Others become landlords by accident, by inheriting a few properties and converting them to rental units. We all have to deal with tenants, enforce payments and perform scheduled maintenance work. The property won't maintain itself and someone has to make the insurance and tax payments.

The landlord life is not a straight path, and we're driven into it for many reasons. If you want to retire, you will have to invest more in the property because the property has to be rentable over an extended period such as over multiple decades. For this purpose, you should purchase the newest and most expensive property possible. If you want to become wealthy and you don't plan to hold out to properties for too long, you can purchase semi run-down properties and make a higher markup renting them out. The following mindset tricks will be detrimental to your success in the rental property business:

1) The Cash Flow Mindset

The most essential landlord mindset is to develop an emergency cash-flow mindset. The faster you gather the cash to purchase the property or put down a deposit, the faster you'll be able to get out of your dead-end 9-5 job and/or retire. Remember you never have to cover the full purchase price of the property and you can get away with paying as little as 20%. If the rental home costs $100,000 you will only have to finance $20,000. How hard is it to save up this amount in today's economy? Even if you live in your mom's basement and work a minimum wage job, you should be able to save up $20,000 and put down a deposit on your first rental property. Don't be afraid to do the dirty jobs and the low-paid jobs because you'll only have to work them until you can finance your first property. Get two jobs! The faster you get the money, the faster you'll be able to finance your properties and create a new life for yourself.

Your focus should be on acquiring as many properties as possible and increasing the cash flow. If you're young and determined, you can afford to do short-term rentals and place an emphasis on increasing cash flow to milk the properties for the maximum amount of dollars viable. If you're reaching retirement age, you need to gather the investment funds you'll need to put down a deposit for stable properties that will pay for your retirement. The landlord mindset is not only about choosing properties and dealing with tenants, it's also about having a sense of urgency and gathering money for new properties. The faster you get at obtaining capital, the more money returns you'll see coming your way.

2) The Enforcer Mindset

The ugly truth about rental properties is that you'll have to deal with real human beings who might not be able to make rent - therefore you'll have to apply discipline and boundaries to make sure you're paid on time. This is especially critical during the first few months when you're getting established and missing a single payment could mean your property is one call away from being repossessed. You'll have to learn how to make your clients pay on time. In effect, you're becoming an enforcer that has to enforce the lease agreement.

What do you do when a tenant misses a payment? The tenant won't care that you have to make mortgage payments on the home; they'll only care for their individual situation. This is why the minute they fail to make a payment, you must file a late rent reminder. This reminder should go out in the first day they don't make a timely payment. The reminder has to have "grace period", which is the time they're allowed to go before they get an eviction warning.

If the tenant fails to pay in the grace period, you should file an eviction notice. The eviction notice notifies the tenant that civil court eviction action will be taken against them. The tenants will come to you with personal stories, but you shouldn't bend and give them leeway because they'll continue asking for more time. If you allow leeway once, they will know that your time is not important. If the landlord doesn't care, why should the tenants pay on time? Only give leeway when you don't have to make mortgage payments or it would compromise your personal relationship with a family member.

1)   The Discipline Mindset

As a landlord you're not only supposed to perform monthly maintenance tasks where you greet your tenants, check up on the property, and collect rent. You must also carry out semi-annual and annual administrative tasks that require discipline and advance planning. What if you get hit with a $4000 bill on a roof leak? You'll need to prepare in advance. This takes discipline. Instead of spending your net profits on cruises in the Caribbean, set them aside for unexpected bills.

The lease terms should be drafted by a lawyer and have a paragraph mentioning a clause for semi-annual inspections which grant you the right to access the property. The properly won't need to have structural damage to warrant an inspection. The landlord shouldn't wait for things to go wrong before inspecting a property. Identify problems in advance and fix them! Make sure that your values are communicated clearly. If you don't tolerate smoking inside the property, you have to be prepared to evict a tenant if you detect smoke. Better yet, get a non-smoker tenant while you're signing the agreement.

Regular maintenance ensures that the property is well-mainlined and that your tenants don't experience problems inhabiting the property. The inspection is not only for property damage but unauthorized pets and people living on the property. While you're carrying out inspections, build up a personal relationship with your tenants. Feel free to ask them about their children, jobs, lives, etc.

Don't forget to raise the rent every year when the lease terms expire. Many landlords worry about raising rents. If you refuse to raise rents, your income will fall behind the market value and won't keep up with inflation. Raise the rents when the lease expires instead of raising it surprisingly at random times during the year, which scares tenants. This way you'll give them the option to pay higher rent prices or find a new property.

Chapter 2—Great Location, Great Investment

Now that we've given you a brief understanding of rental property investments, it's time to tell you about the different classes of real estate, what kinds of properties you can invest in, how you can evaluate target neighborhoods, and how you can identify emerging real estate markets that can generate large profits.

Classes of Real Estate, Where You Should Invest.

If you're going to get involved in the real estate market, you're going to need to familiarize yourself with the way different properties are classified or grouped. Although these classifications are somewhat subjective and there are no universal classifications or guidelines for how to identify properties, we can offer you some guidelines which should be helpful to you in grading specific locations or buildings. Real estate is often classified or graded similar to the way many of us were graded in high school or college, a letter grading system. These grading systems can go from A to C, A to D, A to F. A is obviously the highest rating; F is the poorest rating.

With real estate, the location often receives one rating and the building receives another rating. For example, if you have a great building in a mediocre area, you would have an A building in a C area. If you have an uninhabitable building in a questionable area, you would have an F building in a D area. Following are descriptions on how most people categorize locations with this grading system.

An A location is in an area with the newest buildings, the hottest restaurants, and the best schools. You get the picture. It is an area that will have the highest rents.

An A building is a building that is most likely less than 10 years old. These buildings are likely to have the latest in granite countertops, hardwood floors, etc.

Rental properties in these A areas are likely to be high rent, low maintenance properties. They're easy investments, however it should also be noted that they may also bring a lower return on investment because of the higher demand and higher purchase price.

The B location is often in an area that has decent restaurants, albeit not the trendiest or most expensive restaurants. The schools are good, but not the brand new schools that some of the posh areas have. The area is home to mostly middle class, certainly more blue collar than the A areas. The people living in the B areas are much more likely to be living check to check.

The buildings in the B location are older, usually 15 to 30 years old. Most of these buildings have been upgraded, however not with the amenities of the A buildings.

As an investor in B properties, you'll find that they're likely to require more maintenance and attention than an A property would require. These properties will rent for less than A properties, but they are also capable of bringing you larger profits, because of the more moderate purchase price.

The C locations are marginal locations, often locations that are 30 years or older. The C buildings are often outdated and antiquated, in need of many and frequent repairs. C buildings often require plumbing and electrical upgrades; these buildings often require lots of attention and tender loving care. The upside of these C buildings is that they can often be purchased at a very moderate price; the downside is the amount of money you will likely have to spend to maintain or upgrade them.

D locations are dilapidated areas, often crime-infested and possibly dangerous. These are areas with many vacant or boarded up buildings. The buildings there are either neglected or uninhabitable. Unless you are a seasoned real estate investor, you'll probably want to stay away from investing in these areas. You would really have to know what you're doing to make money from a D building in a D area.

An F building and/or an F location can best be identified as a war zone. Crime-infested, drug-infested, struggling schools, homes and apartments in complete disrepair, etc. You get the picture; nothing that you should be interested in as a novice real estate investor.

Four Important Factors for Evaluating a Neighborhood.

Now that we've outlined the different classes of real estate, it's time to take a look at the different factors involved in evaluating the locations or areas in which you should invest. You've probably heard it before…there three major factors in real estate success: location, location, and location. Yes, that's an old cliché, but it still rings true. Location is almost always going to be the most important factor in the profitability of your real estate investments.

Most rental property investor newbies invest in properties which are near where they live. They do this because they are already familiar with the area, and also because properties in the near vicinity offer easy access for many of the responsibilities involved in rental property: showing the property, maintaining the property, rent collection, etc. Although owning rental property in the same area you live is most advantageous, there is a possible downside. If the economy in your area declines or tanks, you'll have all your eggs in one basket. If all your properties are in one area, they'll all be subject to the same factors which could affect the devaluation of the property, including a declining economy, increasing crime rates, weather disaster events (flooding, tornadoes and hurricanes, earthquakes), etc.

Here are some of the major factors for evaluating an area for possible rental property investment:

1) **Employment rate.** What's the employment rate in the area in which you are thinking of investing? That will have a major impact on how successful you can be with a rental property in that area. Obviously, if the unemployment rate in that area is high, you may find that it's an area in which it's going to be difficult to find and maintain reputable renters.

2) **Crime rate.** The crime rate in the area is also going to be a factor in whether you're going to be able to secure and keep renters. Major crimes such as homicides, sexual assaults, burglaries, robberies, and auto theft are certain to tarnish the reputation and livability of an area and those crimes and the reputation that follows them may impact your chance for success in that area or location.

3) **School system.** Does the area you're considering have a good school system? If you are going to be renting to families with kids, the school system in the area may impact your ability to rent a property. If the area has a good school system, you're likely to find that people will want to live in that area because of that. On the other hand, if the reputation of the area school system is lacking, you may find that people are looking to move out of the district.

4) **Vacancy/No Vacancy.** Is the area you're considering for rental property an area that has a lot of vacancies? Or are there barely any vacancies? This will also be an indicator of the possible success you might have in the area. If there are a lot of vacancies in your area, commercial and residential, you're going to find it much more difficult to rent a property in that area. And you're likely to find that rental rates have much lower profit margins, as the market is much more competitive. If you drive through the neighborhood and find that many businesses or homes are boarded up or vacant, that's not a good sign. On the other hand, if you drive through the area and find that many residences or businesses are remodeling, that's a sign that people are investing in the area.

How to Spot an Emerging Real Estate Market.

If you're going to invest in rental properties, you're going to want to look for emerging real estate markets instead of submerging real estate markets. There are a number of sure indicators as to whether a market is flourishing or struggling. Although a lot of this information can be found online, you should not underestimate the value of finding out information on these areas by simply visiting the area and by meeting with the people who live and work in the area. Although data and analytics are important in making real estate decisions, you should never disregard the "eye test" as part of your decision making.

One determinant to consider in your real estate investments is the population growth of the area. Is the area growing, is it stable or stagnant, is it declining? Obviously, population growth and the corresponding demand for housing is desirable for real estate investors. You'll likely want to tie yourself to an area that is growing in selecting the areas in which you own real estate.

Another factor to consider is existing home sales. Even if an area appears to be economically depressed, an increase in existing home sales can be a strong indicator that an area is reemerging or coming back. As a real estate investor, you need to be aware that areas and neighborhoods often regenerate themselves and if you can get into these areas early in the process, you'll stand to make a lot more profit than you would if you are a latecomer. That being said, some areas and neighborhoods never regenerate and it will be important for you to identify these areas as you decide whether or not to invest in them. Existing home sales within the area are a key indicator to the possible vitality of the area. When reviewing statistics for any area, it is important to note that you'll need to fine tune these statistics as much as possible. For example, if you are looking at making a real estate investment in the Atlanta area, it's important for you to refine that information to a smaller area. Atlanta is a large metropolitan area and there are neighborhoods within that area that are flourishing and other neighborhoods that are struggling at any given time. So, you will need to certainly refine your information search down to a zip code or preferably even a neighborhood within a zip code.

Rising rental rates are another strong indicator in spotting an emerging real estate market. If rental rates are increasing steadily year after year, this is an indication that the real estate market within the area is healthy and a possible target for investment. If you're interested in determining rental rates in a given area, Zillow's rent index provides valuable information, including the median estimated market rate rent across any specific region and housing type.

Also, new construction within an area is an indicator that the area is healthy from a real estate standpoint. The Residential Construction Index provided by the U.S. Census Bureau contains valuable information about the number of building permits which are issued for a particular area and also the number of new homes which are started and completed each month.

Foreclosure rates within any given area are another indicator of real estate investment potential. As someone interested in rental property, you'll probably want to steer clear of areas that have increasing foreclosure rates.

Also, there are less conventional factors which might indicate whether an area is a good target for investment. Has a large company announced that it is relocating to the area or that it is opening a branch in the area? If so, it follows that the employees at this new location will be relocating also. Some of them will be looking to move closer to their workplace. Either way, that can only be good for the economy of the area. On the downside, has a large employer announced that they will be leaving the area? If so, this move is likely to have a negative impact on the local economy.

Another less conventional indicator of real estate rental potential is to determine the normal amount of time it takes for a house to be sold or rented. If that average time frame is over six months, that may well be an indicator that the market is flat and not a good candidate for current investment. On the other hand, if those homes are selling or renting in 30 days, that is a very good sign and it's an indicator that the area is a good investment target.

Chapter 3—Choosing the Best Property

Now that you know more about how to evaluate properties and areas and how to identify areas that are good investment targets, it's time to talk about how to choose the types of real estate investments which will work best for you. This is an important part of the process, as some retail estate investor wannabes make the mistake of choosing an area of real rental that does not fit their interests or their personality.

Residential Real Estate to Invest In

You may be surprised to learn that there are many different types of real estate to invest in, including a number of different types of residential real estate:

1) **Single family homes.** These are the most popular type of rental homes. Although single family homes also include some of the other types of homes listed below (apartment, condos, townhomes, coops, luxury homes, vacation homes), single family homes are the largest category of residential real estate.

2) **Condominiums/coops.** Although condos and coops are single family homes, they are a bit different in that they are managed by a homeowner's association. The homeowner's association is often responsible for the common areas and responsibilities for the complex, including garbage collection, landscaping, common area maintenance, and often exterior maintenance of the individual units. In return, the homeowner's association collects a fee from all members. If you are going to rent out a unit that is managed by a homeowner's association, you'll have to incorporate the homeowner's fees into the rent amount you charge your tenants.

3) **Multi-family homes.** Multi-family units are properties that include two or more dwellings which are rented out separately. This includes apartment building, duplexes, and triplexes. With some real estate investors, the owner is living in one of the units and is then renting out the other units. Owning multi-family homes is slightly more complicated than owning single family homes, as the performance of the property is based on the performance of each unit individually. Also, you should know that multi-family homes are sometimes classified as commercial properties, depending on the number of units involved.

4) **Luxury homes.** Luxury homes are top-quality homes which contain the latest amenities, technologies, and appliances. These are properties that demand top-dollar rental rates. And they are the most expensive homes to invest in.

5) **Vacation homes.** Vacation homes are often rented out on a seasonal basis, with the rental rates fluctuating from high during the peak season to lower during non-peak season. Most vacation homes are located in tourist areas. Areas in Texas, Florida, and Arizona have plenty of vacation homes to accommodate "snowbirds", people from northern areas of the U.S. trying to escape the cold weather and snow of the winters. Investors also own vacation homes along the coasts in various locations. Others own vacation homes near tourist destinations such as Disney World. And lake homes in the northern areas of the country such as Minnesota, Michigan, and Wisconsin, can also be good investments. One of the advantages of owning a vacation property is that the owners will often use these properties for their own vacations or getaways and then rent out the property for the remainder of the year.

Types of Commercial Real Estate

Commercial real estate covers a lot of different types of real estate, all the way from single office buildings or spaces to massive skyscrapers, airports, stadiums, amusement parks, and shopping malls. As a real estate rental newbie, we're going to presume that you're closer to the lower end of investors, but you should know that almost all of the types of commercial real estate we're listing include both small and large properties. Because of the costs involved, commercial real estate is almost always a higher stakes game. By the same token, most commercial leases are longer than residential leases, because of the accommodations which are normally made to the building or the property for the tenants.

1) **Office space.** This is the most common commercial property. The office space spectrum ranges from single tenant properties to skyscrapers and office complexes which are home to hundreds of tenants and thousands of their employees. Like residential properties, commercial properties are classified on grade levels (i.e.—A, B, C). Class A commercial real estate consists of new buildings or recently refurbished/extensively refurbished buildings. They are normally in excellent areas and normally managed by professional management companies. Class B commercial real estate is the most popular class for investors. Class B properties are generally slightly older buildings that require some capital investment for minor repairs or upgrades. Class C commercial properties are often old buildings that are targeted for major renovations or redevelopment. Those who invest in Class C properties can generally expect major capital investments to bring the property up-to-date and to make it marketable to tenants. Vacancy rates are usually much higher for Class C properties and these properties are much more difficult to lease.

2) **Retail.** Again, the spectrum range is huge, ranging from a print shop that might have two or three employees to a restaurant or bank

that might have 50 employees to a huge shopping mall that might have thousands of employees. Retail properties are often located in urban areas or business districts. Most shopping malls are owned by large investment groups, but on the lower end of the spectrum, some of the smaller retail locations are owned by single, mom-and-pop, or family investors.

3)   **Industrial.** Industrial properties range from manufacturing facilities to warehouse facilities. They often require larger amounts of space to accommodate dock areas for shipments that come in and go out. These industrial properties are generally in lower rent, lower traffic areas, as they are lower profile businesses that do not require prime real estate.

4)   **Multi-family.** This includes residential locations that have as few as four units. It also includes large apartment complexes and high-rise condominium complexes. Many residential property investors who want to get into commercial real estate choose to get into commercial real estate by investing in multi-family properties such as apartment buildings that can accommodate anywhere from four to a dozen tenants. As we discuss commercial real estate in this chapter, it should be pointed out that residential leases are often much shorter than commercial leases. Most residential leases have six or 12-month terms. Most commercial leases will range from three to 20 years, depending on the building and the business. Commercial leases are normally longer because the owner often has to make accommodations to the building in order to fit the tenant's business. And then when that tenant leaves, the building or space generally has to be repurposed or remodeled to fit the next tenant.

5)   **Special purpose.** As long as we just mentioned repurposing, we should also mention special purpose commercial real estate. This is generally a building that is built for a unique or special purpose and

can not often be repurposed without a lot of renovation. Businesses such as car washes, schools, and storage facilities are considered special purpose locations. For example, if you own a property and are leasing to a tenant who has a car wash, it's not going to be easy to repurpose that building if and when the tenant leaves. You're either going to have to lease to another tenant who wants to use the facility as a car wash or you're going to have to be prepared to make major accommodations or renovations for the next tenant. That's why leases for special purpose buildings are generally much longer than leases for other types of commercial real estate.

And while we're discussing special purpose commercial real estate, we should also mention mixed use developments. These developments have become extremely popular in recent years, mostly in urban areas. An example of a mixed use development would be a multiple story apartment complex with a business or businesses on the ground floor. That business might be a pizza restaurant, a health club, or even a supermarket. Generally, the business located on the ground floor of the complex is a retail location which can benefit financially from the tenants above. Along the same lines, large corporations have mixed use buildings in which their offices constitute a large amount of the space, but then they lease the remaining space to other retail businesses who can benefit from the large number of employees. As an example, a large corporation in the electronics industry has a campus with multiple buildings and thousands of employees. They allow certain retail companies to rent space within their building, including coffee companies, a dry cleaners, a health club, and a doctor's office. The feeling is that not only can these businesses benefit from the corporation's large numbers of employees, the corporation is also making things more convenient for employees who no longer need to leave the premises for some of their errands or activities.

6) **Owner occupied.** Some real estate investors purchase property with the intent of using it for their own purposes. And some of these investors will use a portion of the space for themselves and then rent out other portions to tenants. This strategy can be applied to many of the commercial real estate options discussed above.

The 1% Rule for Investing in Real Estate

We previously mentioned the 1% Rule. As you consider which real estate investments to make, you'll need to use some kind of measurement tool to determine how much rent you would need to charge for a property, commercial or residential. You'll need to make sure that the rent you are charging your tenants will at least cover all of your expenses for the property; hopefully more, so you can make a profit. After all, most of us do not intend to get into the real estate business as a hobby; most of us are looking to make a profit. The 1% rule for investing is one way you can determine how much rent you'll need to charge for any rental property you invest in. Here's how it works. (Excuse us for being a bit redundant, but it's absolutely imperative that you have a measurement tool for the amount of rent you'll need to charge to derive income from the property.)

With the 1% rule, you simply multiply the purchase price of the property by 1% to determine the base level of the monthly rent you will need to charge. For example, if you purchase a property for $300,000, you'll multiply that by 1% to get a base rate of $3000. That $3000 will be the base you should work from in determining a rent level from a tenant. But please know that this is just the base level and you will also need to consider other expenses for the property, including things such as insurance, taxes, and upkeep. Upkeep can include things such as garbage collection, janitorial services, snow removal, and landscaping. Those expenses will also need to be accounted for as you work to determine your rent level and your break-even point.

Obviously, the rent or rents you are charging need to cover your mortgage payments (unless you are indeed investing in real estate as a charity or a hobby.) If the property you are interested in will require any major repairs or renovations before it can be leased, you'll need to add those cost estimates to the purchase price before you calculate the 1%. For example, if the $300,000 property you're interested in will require a $20,000 roof repair before it is marketable, you'll add that $20,000 before you divide by 1%. As an investor, you should ideally seek a mortgage loan with monthly payments that are less than the 1% figure you've calculated.

Again, there are many other factors to consider in evaluating the profit potential of a property, but the 1% rule at least gives you a base to work from in determining what rent level you would need to charge and what kind of mortgage payments you should look for in purchasing the property.

Essential Questions to Keep in Mind When Evaluating Property

Investing in real estate for rental is a major consideration and you'll need to make sure you ask yourself the correct questions in evaluating any property. Here are some questions you should be asking as you consider purchasing rental properties:

1) **Will the location make for a solid investment?** As mentioned before, location might be the major factor in whether a rental property is profitable. In evaluating any location, there are a number of things to consider. Is the location near to amenities that your prospective tenants are going to require? If you're planning to rent to young families with kids, nearby amenities such as good

schools, supermarkets, gyms, and restaurants will enhance your investment. If you are planning to rent to senior citizens, nearby amenities such as supermarkets, doctors' offices and medical clinics, and health clubs will be attractive to prospective renters. If you are thinking of renting to college students, nearby bars, restaurants, and gyms may enhance the attractiveness of your property. Another thing to consider with location is whether the area contains a large enough pool of prospective renters. For example, if you have an upscale property in an area where mostly middle class workers reside, you may have difficulty renting that property. If you have a low-rent Class C property in an area that is predominantly upscale residents, you may have difficulty renting. So, make sure that your location matches the pool of prospective renters you're targeting. If you can make sure your pool of prospective tenants matches your property, you'll ensure that you have consistent rental income over the time you own the property.

2)   Is the property functional? If not, what's it going to take to make it functional? It's okay to buy a property that needs repairs, even major repairs. However, before you purchase such a property, you'll have to determine how much it's going to cost and how long it's going to take to make the property functional. Novice investors are notorious for underestimating the costs involved in fixing up a property. We've heard some people say that if you are estimating costs and time frame for a property you should simply take whatever figures you come up with and double them. They live by the mantra, "If something can go wrong, it's likely to go wrong." So, if they have calculated renovation costs of $20,000, they'll be thinking that they could end up spending up to $40,000 for the renovation. If they calculate six weeks to do the renovation, they'll be aware that they renovation could take up to three months if things don't go as planned.

In evaluating the property you're interested in, you will have to determine what items you can fix yourself and what items you'll have to hire contractors for. And then you'll have to secure quotes for the work from those contractors. And obviously, you'll also have to price out materials costs for any renovation. This can be a somewhat complicated process; that's why many novice rental real estate investors will opt to purchase properties which do not require major renovations. They'll take the attitude that at least they have a better indication of what they are getting into as far as costs are concerned. If you're not experienced in renovating properties, you're more likely to stumble upon some expensive surprises in fixing up a property.

Also, you should know that when we are referring to a functional property, we are also referring to a property that is easily rentable to tenants and one that is safe for tenants. If these things aren't happening, you'll limit your ability to rent the property or you may endanger a tenant to the point where you are risking their safety or risking a serious insurance claim against you. For example, if you have a leaky roof, that will almost surely impact your ability to rent the property or, even, if you rent it, may jeopardize your ability to keep renting the property. Or, if your roof is in total disrepair, you might actually endanger the safety of a tenant.

3) **What's it going to cost to maintain the property?** In evaluating the viability or possible profitability of a rental property, you'll also need to determine what it is going to cost to maintain it. For example, if you own a small office complex, you're probably going to have to pay for landscaping and garbage collection. If you have common areas in the building, you'll have to pay for janitorial services, including restroom maintenance. If you're in a northern area, you'll probably have to pay for snow plowing or removal. All of these maintenance costs will have an impact on the profitability of your rental property. And you should note that there may be more costs involved in some rentals than in others. For example, if you are renting out a vacation property that turns over tenants frequently, you'll have to pay more to frequently prepare the property for new tenants. If you are renting a property to college students who may use it as a party

house, you may have to pay higher damage or repair costs as you prepare for new tenants. Is the property close to where you are living or working? Will you be willing to make any minor repairs yourself or will you need to hire a management company to handle these repairs? Those are all things to think about when you are evaluating the viability of a rental property.

Besides repair and routine maintenance costs, you'll have to ask yourself some other questions regarding the viability of the property. What are the expected property taxes? Projected insurance costs? What are the vacancy rates for the area the property is located in? How will you accommodate vacancy expenses? Will you have a separate fund set up for that or will you have to borrow money for that? (Hopefully, not the latter.) Is the rent amount you'll have to charge for the property competitive with rates being charged for similar properties in the same area? Is the property locating in a flourishing area? Declining area? Are there any changes coming to the area that will impact the economy? (i.e.—A major company coming to the area or leaving the area? Light rail or other major transportation routes coming to the area? A sports stadium coming to the area? This might impact parking availability in the area and make a residential property less desirable. On the other hand, it might also offer more opportunities in regards to commercial real estate for new restaurants, bars, and hotels.

Buying an investment property can be complicated. The upside is that rental property can also be very profitable. But you'll want to make sure that you've asked yourself all the necessary questions before you invest in any property. Miscalculating any of these factors could well make the difference between being profitable or losing money on your investment.

Chapter 4—Financing Your Rental Property

We've been talking about why owning rental property is a good idea, the different types of rental property investments to consider, and things to consider in choosing a rental property. Now it's time to tell you about the ways you can finance a rental property. There are multiple ways to do this, including some ways for first-time investors to enter the market.

House Hacking: Make Money and Live for Free

Some of you may not be familiar with the term "house hacking", so before we get into how to do it, we should explain what it is. House hacking involves the renting or leasing of owner-occupied properties to tenants in an effort to subsidize the occupany costs for the owner. House hacking is particularly popular with young, single investors. Here's how it works. A person will purchase a home (or office location) with the intention to live in that home. They'll then rent that home out to one or more occupants and use that rental income to subsidize or finance the cost of the property. As an example, a recent college grad opts to buy a starter home and then share it with two roommates. His mortgage payment is $1100 a month and he charges each of his roommates $600 a month in rent to cover the cost of his mortgage and some of the additional costs of the house, including water and electric. In essence, the recent college grad is able to live in the home for free, and at the same time, have his tenants pay for the equity he accumulates in the home.

The upside for the roommates is that they pay less to live in his home than they would to rent a one bedroom apartment. At the same time, they have more space and possibly more amenities than they would get with a one bedroom apartment.

The possible downside to the owner is that he has share his living quarters and he may prefer more privacy. (On the other hand, he may enjoy the company.) As most of us who have shared a living area know, the living arrangement will work much better if the parties are compatible. Also, there may be some security risks if you rent to a stranger. We've heard the story of a man who shared his home with a roommate, only to come home one day to find that all of his major belongings had disappeared.

It should also be pointed out that house hacking doesn't always involve roommates. It's not uncommon for some house hackers to purchase duplexes or triplexes, living in one of the units and then renting out the other units to others. This affords the owner a lot more privacy than he would receive in sharing a unit with roommates.

Let's outline the benefits of house hacking:

1) **You can decrease or eliminate your housing expense.** As you all know, for most of us, our housing expensive is usually our largest monthly expense. Statistics show that Americans spend about 40% of their income on housing. In house hacking, you will be able to substantially reduce or eliminate those expenses. And for the recent college grads who are living with parents, house hacking also offers more independence than you'll have cohabiting with your parents.

2) **Increase your income, savings.** Many people look at the house hacking stage as a transitional stage or temporary stage which allows them to work toward their own financial independence while they pay off school or car loans or save money toward the next home after the starter home. Some people will house hack as they work toward a second investment property; others will simply use the money to pay for a nice vacation.

3) Get some experience as a landlord. Living with tenants will allow you to get your feet wet in the world of being a landlord. In listening to the wants, needs, and concerns of your tenants, you'll get an inkling of what it's like to be a landlord. You'll also get an inkling of the things that can go wrong for a landlord (roof leaks, tenant late on the rent, refrigerator stops working, etc.). When repairs are required, you'll learn to solve problems, either by repairing the items yourself or enlisting someone to do the repairs for you.

4) Owning property. In owning property as a house hacker, you'll be establishing equity on the property. At the same time, your investment value may be escalating and when you go to sell the property, you'll reap the benefits of the escalated value.

Creative Ways to Finance Your Rental Properties

The conventional way to purchase a rental property is to save up for the down payment and then secure a mortgage to cover the remaining amount. There are however some other ways you can finance the purchase of a rental property.

1) House Hacking. As outlined above, house hacking is a popular way to finance your first rental property.

2) Seller Financing. Some sellers are willing to loan money for the purchase of their property. Some of them are willing to loan the entire amount of the purchase; others are willing to loan the down payment amount. If you can do this, you might find that it is a much simpler process than a bank loan with less paperwork. As someone who is buying the property, you'll want to make sure that you are getting a fair interest rate for the purchase. Unless you're very experienced in purchasing real estate properties, you will be well advised to consult with an attorney and/or CPA in initiating this purchase. And whatever you do, make sure you get your agreement in writing. For many of you, this will be one of the largest purchases of your life and you will certainly want to make sure that it is properly documented.

In discussing seller financing, you should know that many sellers do not advertise that they offer financing. If you are truly interested in seller financing as an option, you should ask the seller if they are willing to offer financing. It's possible that the seller hasn't thought about this before and you may find that they are so interested to sell the property that they will be willing to offer you financing at a good rate.

3) **Partnerships.** If you don't have enough money for a down payment, you might secure a partner in your purchase. Do you have a friend or family member who would be willing to partner with you in purchasing a rental property? Although you can structure a partnership agreement any way you want, you should know that with a lot of real estate partnership agreements, one partner will make the down payment and then the other partner will handle all of the landlord duties, including collecting rent, making or arranging repairs, corresponding with tenants, etc. In essence, the person making the down payment is generally a silent partner. In return for the down payment, the two partners then agree to split the profits derived from the rental income and also when the property is sold. Again, these partnership agreements can be structured any way you and your partner want, but the basic tenet of the partnership is that one partner will provide the funds while the other will do the work.

Many partnerships are limited liability companies (LLCs) in which you can specifically outline your agreement and the corresponding roles and responsibilities of each party. LLCs are great in that they will also allow you to protect your personal assets in the event your business or partnership is ever sued. As we recommend previously in regards to seller financing, all partnership agreements should be outlined in writing. Verbal agreements and handshake agreements are not advised for such a major purchase. If you don't have a relationship with an attorney who can initiate an LLC or partnership agreement for you, companies such as Rocket Lawyer or LegalZoom are available online to help you draft simple legal agreements.

4) **Government programs.** You may or may not be familiar with FHA, the Federal Housing Administration. The FHA offers reasonable loans for owner-occupied properties, including single homes, duplexes, triplexes, and quadruplexes or four-unit apartment buildings. The loan rate for FHA loans is very reasonable at 3-1/2%. Loan limits for FHA loans are different in every county, so, if you're interested in FHA financing, we suggest that you find out what the loan limit is in your county before you get too far along in your search for rental investment properties.

5) **Retirement accounts.** If you're a bit older and you have some retirement accounts you can draw from, this is another good way to finance the purchase of a rental property. If you have a self-directed IRA (Individual Retirement Account), you're not restricted to traditional assets such as stocks or mutual funds. You're also allowed to invest those funds in non-traditional assets, including rental property. Again, we're going to suggest that you consult with a professional in using retirement accounts funds for a real estate purchase, whether that is a financial planner or a certified public accountant. Purchasing a rental property is serious business and you should not try to do so without professional counsel, unless you are experienced at doing so.

Start Saving for a Down Payment Right Now

As someone who is already this far into the book, it seems as if you have a sincere interest in purchasing and owning a rental property. That being said, you may be asking yourself how in the world you're ever going to accumulate the amount you'll need to actually purchase that property. In this chapter, we've outlined some simple thoughts on how you can save enough money to make a down payment. Most of these ideas are financial planning techniques that can be successful for anyone who is looking to save enough money for any particular purchase.

1) **The Percentage Plan.** In using the percentage plan, we encourage you first to determine where all of your income is normally being spent. We suggest that you detail all of your mandatory or fixed expenditures within the past 90 days. Mandatory or fixed expenditures will be payments you have to make and will include things such as rent, utilities, school and car loans, food, gas, cable television, internet services, cell phone, etc. These payments should be easy to track, as you'll have receipts for most of them. Although some of these payments will vary slightly from month to month (i.e.—Your electric bill might be $60 one month and $70 another month), you should have enough information to figure out what your average monthly expenditure is. You'll then place all of these mandatory or fixed expenses in one category and move to the next category, which we'll call discretionary spending.

Discretionary spending covers remaining expenses that aren't necessary expenditures—things such as health club or gym memberships, the daily cup of joe you get from your neighborhood coffee shop, bar/restaurant/entertainment expenses, weekend getaways and vacations, etc. After you've listed all of the discretionary expenditures you can remember, you should then review these expenditures and see if any of them could be eliminated without severely cramping your lifestyle. Are you using your gym membership? Can you do without the daily cup of coffee from the neighborhood coffee shop? Do you really need to eat at restaurants three times a week? Can you do without a weekend getaway? Do you really need the premium cable tv package or could you make do with the less expensive basic package? In listing all of your discretionary expenses for the past 90 days, you'll be able to see how you are spending your money. If you can eliminate or reduce any of your discretionary expenditures, you should then be able to allocate these funds toward saving for a rental property down payment.

After you've totaled your fixed expenditures and determined what your discretionary expenditures should be, you should calculate what portion of your income each of these two categories accounts for. Most people find that fixed expenditures account for anywhere from 50 to 70 percent of their income. Your fixed expenditures are mostly non-negotiable. Maybe you can cut a small amount off your cable tv package by dropping some of the premium channels. Maybe you can carpool or consolidate your errands to save on gas expenditures. But for the most part, your fixed expenditures are what they are.

Your discretionary expenditures are exactly as described...they're discretionary. You should determine exactly which of these expenditures you can't do without and which of those you could either eliminate or reduce. After you've determined the amount you want to allocate on a monthly basis for discretionary activities, you should then see what percentage of your income these expenditures entail. And then see how much is left over for savings.

Some people will end up with a 70/20/10 plan. (70% fixed, 20% discretionary, 10% savings.) Others will end up with a 50/30/20 plan. You'll go with whatever works best for you, however the important thing is the savings category, as you'll use those funds to make the down payment on your rental property.

In setting a monthly limit for you discretionary spending, you will be able to save an accumulate the funds necessary to purchase your rental property. Are you an impulse spender? If so, you're the type of person who is likely to have the most difficulty in controlling your discretionary spending. If this is the case and you need help in controlling your monthly expenditures, there are apps that can help you do so. *Mint* is a popular app which can help you with your discretionary spending by alerting you when you are nearing the monthly limit you've assigned to your discretionary spending. When you get a "warning" that you're near your limit, maybe that warning will help you dial back your Amazon purchases or your Starbuck's coffee purchases.

Again, there's no set rule on how to set up your own income percentage plan. Whatever works for you should be fine, as long as you're setting aside a monthly amount you'll need for the down payment on your rental property.

2)   Reverse Engineer. Another way you can determine how long it's going to take you to save for your rental property down payment is to work backwards using reverse engineering. In doing so, you'll first determine the approximate price of the property you'll be looking to buy. For purposes of this example, we'll use $100,000 as the number to work with. We realize that this number may be extremely low for certain areas of the country, but it is an easy number to work with, especially for the mathematically impaired. Ha.

So, if, for example, you're thinking of purchasing a $100,000 property, you'll know that you'll have a 20% down payment on that property ($20,000). In addition to the down payment, you'll have closing costs that normally range from 1-2% of the down payment. You'll also need a contingency fund of maybe another 1-2%. For purposes of this example, let's keep it simple and list both the closing costs and the contingency/rainy day fund at $2000 each. So, coupled with the $20,000 down payment, you will need approximately $24,000 to purchase a $100,000 property. If you want to purchase the rental property in two years, you'll then divide the $24,000 total amount by

24 months. This will show you that you will need to save $1000 a month to reach your two-year savings goal. If this is too ambitious, you can always change your savings plan from 24 to 30 or 36 months. Or you can make the decision to look for less expensive/lower-priced properties. Again, there is no set prescription for how to establish a savings plan. You'll have to decide what works best for you or what you can live with. The goal of these savings plans is simply to get you to do the math in determining what it will take to accumulate the funds to purchase a rental property and then to put a plan into action.

3) **Automate Your Budget.** It's no secret that lack of will power is the most common deterrent to any budget. You resolve to control your spending at the beginning of the month and then a few days into the month you find the signed National Football League jersey you've been looking for on ebay or the designer bag you've been looking for on Amazon. So much for the budget you set up at the start of the month. Five days in and you've already blown your discretionary budget limit. If this is you and if you have difficulty controlling impulse purchases, you might consider automating your payments, especially your savings payments.

If, after reviewing your expenditures, you've determined that you can save $750 a month, go ahead a set up an automatic payment once or twice a month from your checking account to a separate savings account you've designated for your rental property purchase. You should have a good idea as to when you get paid and you'll know whether you get paid monthly or semi-monthly. Set up the automated deposits to your savings account soon after your paychecks are deposited. Maybe a day or two after. At the same time, set up all of your other fixed expenditures to be paid automatically at the same time, possibly on the same days. Then whatever funds are left in your account that month, you'll be able to use as you see fit for your discretionary purchases. In setting up automated payments, you'll make sure that all of your fixed expenses are paid. You'll also be safeguarding the amounts you want going into savings, as those amounts will be deposited before you make any discretionary purchases.

As mentioned earlier in this chapter, we suggest that you review all of your expenditures before you set up any budget plan and then determine if there are any areas which you can eliminate or reduce expenditures. Cut out the things which are not adding value to your life.

Chapter 5—Real Estate Tools for Success

Now that you know how to accumulate the funds you'll need to make the down payment on your first rental property, let's expand the picture and talk about some ways you can build a real estate portfolio and the people you'll want to have on your real estate "team" if you have multiple properties.

Strategies for Building a Successful Rental Property Portfolio.

One of the main reasons the real estate rental market is so attractive is because home ownership is dwindling and the percentage of people who are renting is increasing. That's been happening for a couple of decades now, and with the price of homes continuing to rise, that trend probably won't change any time soon. With this in mind, it's a great time to invest in real estate rental properties and establish a portfolio of profitable properties that will leave you financially set for the rest of your life. Here are a number of different ways you can establish your real estate portfolio past your first rental property:

1) **Buy Multi-Family Units.** We've detailed many of the benefits of multi-family units previously in this book. If you want to build your real estate "empire", one of the best ways to do that is to start purchasing multi-family units. Real estate investment newbies often start with owner-occupied multi-family units such as duplexes, triplexes, and quadruplexes; they then graduate to larger multi-family units such as apartment complexes. In owning multiple units at the same location, you'll be able to consolidate your efforts and costs. An owner who has four single family rental homes will obviously have to put in a lot more time, effort, and running around than an owner who owns a quadruplex. So, if you want to start expanding your real estate rental empire, multi-family properties are a great place to start.

2) **The Snowball Method.** Warren Buffet is one of the most successful investors of all time and he has had a lot of success using the snowball method of investing. Most of us who live in the northern areas of the US are familiar with how to build a snowball; some of you in the South may never have experienced snow. So, I'll remind you how a snowball is made. You start with a small ball of snow that often fits in your hand. As you roll that snowball along the snow-covered ground, it gathers additional snow and the ball gets bigger and bigger. We've seen instances of people who make snowballs taller than they are.

The same goes with the snowball method of investing. Instead of using the profits from your first rental property to buy new vehicles or to take luxurious vacations, you can use that profit toward the purchase of another property. Many investors use this philosophy (and some of them don't even know it). It's a great way to expand a real estate empire and, if your properties are profitable, you'll surely find that you'll pick up momentum as you go along. And you'll have a much wider selection of properties to choose to invest in as you make more money. You'll be able to graduate from one single family home or a duplex into multiple single family homes or multi-unit properties, including apartment complexes. So, you'll be wise to let the money you make from your rental property investments work for you. Instead of using those profits solely for personal amenities, you'll be wise to use those funds in other investments.

3) **Start with Partnerships.** We discussed some of the benefits of partnerships in the section on how to secure the money to buy your first rental property. Partnerships can also work well beyond the first property. As you get more heavily into real estate investment, you may want to "up the ante" on the properties you're investing in.

You're likely to want to invest in larger, more expensive units. Having an investment partner will allow you to do this more quickly and it will also reduce your financial exposure on the property you're investing in. Also, as far as financing goes, you may find that the banks that financed your previous mortgages, may eventually be reluctant to provide additional mortgages because they don't want to "have all of their eggs in one basket".

4) **The C-B-A Strategy.** We previously discussed the different classes of real estate. Class A properties are generally the premier properties—new buildings in great areas. Repairs generally not necessary. Class B properties are generally slightly older properties in good areas. Maybe minor repairs necessary. Class C properties are often marginal properties in marginal areas with many minor or even some major repairs required. Many real estate investors who are trying to build a portfolio will start by investing in Class C properties and then work their way up to Class B and then Class A properties. The C properties are less expensive than A properties and they require a lot more work initially. In starting out with C or B properties, you'll quickly get a good education on what it takes to be a successful rental property investor. Then as you accumulate money from these Class C properties, you'll be able to invest in the more expensive Class B or Class A properties. As we say this, you should know that some investors choose to stay mostly in the same class. We know successful investors who stay mostly with Class B properties instead of ever moving to Class A properties because they find the B properties to be more profitable or more plentiful…or they just feel more comfortable in that area. Either way, you get the idea…you have to learn to take baby steps first before you can walk, and you have to learn to walk before you can run.

5) **Mix It Up.** One of the keys to having a successful real estate portfolio is to mix it up…have a diversified portfolio. Some investors get stuck in staying with properties that work for them. Maybe they buy only residential properties and no commercial properties. Maybe they buy only Class B properties. Maybe they buy only properties in the same area of town. Although there is certainly something to be said about staying with what works for you, the "if it ain't broke, don't fix it" approach, there's also something to be said for diversification. We know an investor who for years invested only in properties in a major metropolitan area. These were C properties that the investor purchased and renovated. At the time he started purchasing these properties, that area of the city was revitalizing itself. His investments were extremely profitable and he made a conscious decision never to go outside that area with his real estate investments. Flash forward 20 years after his purchase there. The same area of the city that had once been revitalized was on a severe decline. A middle class/ lower middle class area that had once been moderately safe was now crime-ridden, drug-infested, and dangerous. Schools that were once considered good schools were now considered to be sub-par. Restaurants and other businesses that had previously flourished were struggling, some of them shuttered. The investor's investments were in severe decline, all because he had placed all of his eggs in the same basket and opted not to diversify. Again, no one is telling you that you should abandon the real estate investing philosophy that works for you, but, in the long run, you'll do best if you choose to diversify your investments.

Commercial Real Estate, Another Means to Build Your Portfolio

Commercial real estate is a different ballgame than residential real estate. For obvious reasons, commercial real estate is generally more expensive than residential real estate. Unlike residential real estate, where conventional leases are generally one year, commercial leases usually start at three years and go up to 20 years, depending on how much the property has to be customized for the tenant. If you are a real estate rental newbie, it's unlikely that you'll get into commercial real estate investing in a big way, but we'd nevertheless like to give you a brief capsule explanation of the different categories or strategies of commercial real estate investment.

1) **Core Real Estate Investments.** Core investments are known as the safest commercial real estate investments. With a core investment strategy, investors will look for stable properties in stable areas. This means high quality buildings in low vacancy areas. With a core investment strategy, investors are generally looking yield (immediate payoff) over appreciation (long-term payoff). Return on core real estate investments is generally under 10%, but investors are attracted to this strategy because it is a stable and low risk strategy.

2) **Core-Plus Investments.** As the name indicates, core-plus investments are similar to core investments, however they generally offer an opportunity to enhance returns through minor renovation or repositioning in the marketplace. These are still stable and appealing properties with a slightly higher degree of risk (possibly including some key leases that are near expiration).

3) **Value-Added Investments.** Value-added investments are the most popular strategy for commercial real estate investment. Whereas core investment strategies will normally bring less than 10% return, value-added investments will normally bring 10-15% return. Whereas the goal of a core investment strategy favors yield over appreciation, a value-added investment strategy favors appreciation over yield. In other words, a value-added investor is often OK with not receiving large profits on the property until it is either renovated, repositioned, or sold. A value-added investor is in it for the long haul and will usually hold the assets for at least five to seven years or until they've had time to enhance or reposition the property. The value-added real estate strategy is a higher risk/higher reward strategy.

Lease terms and lease situations are particularly critical with a value-added strategy. For example, let's take an older industrial complex that was built in the 1970s. The complex has 12 tenants, all of whom had five-year leases when they first moved into the complex. 10 of the leases are due to expire within the next 18 months; the other two leases are for newer tenants. The building has three vacancies. Over time, it has become more difficult to lease spaces to tenants as the complex is one of the oldest within what is still a stable area. With this in mind, it looks like this complex offers a great opportunity for renovation or repositioning which would result in higher rents. On the other hand, if most of the tenants had longer times remaining on their leases, it would probably not be a good time to remodel, as you'd be spending significant remodeling dollars on tenants who are already locked into longer-term leases. So, if you're purchasing rental properties with existing tenants, you'll definitely want to take a look at the lease situation for those tenants to make sure that those leases jibe with the plans you have for the property.

4) **Opportunistic.** Investors who use the opportunistic investment strategy are investors who are willing to take the highest risks to achieve the highest rewards. Opportunistic properties include both existing properties and new developments. With the existing properties, those properties usually need significant work. These are normally high vacancy properties that are difficult to lease. These also might be areas that require repurposing or repositioning. As an example, what was once a huge brewery complex dating back to the late 1800s had been vacant for over 10 years after the brewery had been purchased by another brewery and the brewing plants had been consolidated. A group of investors decided to repurpose the main brewhouse as an international market which now has over 30 tenants. Obviously, this was a high risk/high reward situation as the investor group had to pump millions into the repurposing of the building and the complex. But if they are successful in turning their international market into a high-traffic destination, they'll stand to make high rewards for their strategy.

10 People You'll Need on Your Real Estate Dream Team

If you're going to build a successful real estate portfolio, you're going to have to have a "team" of people you can use throughout the process. Being a successful real estate investor requires a lot of different hats. Unlike some other profit ventures, being a "lone wolf" isn't going to work if you're a real estate investor. You're going to need the help and expertise of others in order to be successful. Here are some of the people you'll need on your real estate rental team as you work toward establishing your portfolio.

1) **Banker.** Hopefully, you'll be able to establish a working relationship with a banker and he or she will come to know what you are looking for in a bank loan. Fast closing? Lower interest rates?

2) **Mortgage Broker.** You'll want to find someone who is going to work for you to find the types of mortgage that you're looking for. As with most members on your team, you're going to want someone who understands your business, especially if you are purchasing properties on an on-going basis.

3) **Accountant/Bookkeeper.** You'll need someone who understands real estate, including local and state real estate laws.

4) **Real Estate Attorney.** There are plenty of attorneys out there, but it will behoove you to find an attorney who specializes in real estate. For example, if you have a tenant who is not paying, you'll need an attorney who is familiar with state eviction procedures.

5) **Insurance Agent.** Again, you'll benefit from an agent who is willing to shop for the best policies to fit your needs.

6) **Appraiser.** A good appraiser can not only give you an accurate valuation of your property, they can also suggest ways in which you can increase the value of your property.

7)   Inspector. A good inspector can save you tons of money. If they're thorough, they can tell you exactly what repairs will need to be made in a prospective property and how quickly those repairs will have to be made. A good inspector can be worth his or her weight in gold.

8)   Property Manager. If you own multiple properties or even if you own just one property and don't have the time necessary to accommodate the needs of your tenants, you'll want a good property manager. Good property managers can often mean the difference as to whether your property is rented or vacant, profitable or not profitable.

9)   Real Estate Agent. As you continue to build your portfolio, you'll hopefully be able to establish a solid working relationship with a real estate agent who understands the kinds of properties you are looking for. If they don't have a good idea as to what you're looking for, they'll waste a lot of your time.

10)   Cleaning Person or Crew. Are you going to clean a unit every time it goes vacant? Anyone who has ever done that knows that it can be a lot of work. A good cleaning crew can be a valuable asset to your real estate team.

Again, it's important to note that you should assemble a team that you can use on an on-going basis for you real estate rental properties. In doing so, it will be important for you to communicate to these team members exactly what your wishes are and what you're looking for. If you can do that, they'll became assets for you and you won't have to start at square one every time you have a need for their corresponding services. As with any team, if one of your team members is not meeting your expectations, you'll be better served to find someone else to fill their position. Your success as a real estate investor may well lie in the hands of the real estate team you assemble.

Chapter 6—The Rental to Outshine All Others

So, you're the proud owner of your very first rental property. As expected, it's going to need some work before it's rentable and you'll need to come up with a plan to get the property ready to rent. In this chapter, we'll give you a step-by-step plan on how to rehabilitate a property and get it ready to rent. We'll also tell you about some simple improvements you can make to instantly improve the value or marketability of the property.

10 Steps for Rehabbing Your Rental Property

If you're going to rehab your new rental property, you'll need to come up with a practical plan and schedule for what you're going to do and when you're going to do it. Property owners who do not get organized and instead "fly by the seat of their pants" are setting themselves up for major problems in this process. Also, as you embark on the rehabbing process for your property, you should remember that you may have to remain flexible at times. Murphy's law states that if things can go wrong, they will go wrong and you should not be surprised if you have some hiccups or hit some snags during the process. But hopefully by coming up with a detailed and practical plan before the process begins, you'll be able to minimize any potential problems. Here are some steps you can take in the rehabbing process:

1) **Assess Each Area of the Property.** Hopefully, you'll have done a preliminary assessment before you purchased the property. You'll need to go through each area of the property and determine what needs to be done to a) make the property livable and b) make it more attractive to prospective tenants. This includes a room-by-room assessment of the interior of the property and also an assessment of the exterior of the property. If you have purchased a home with a detached garage, your assessment should include the garage. Your assessment should also include a review of the landscaping and the overall appearance of the property. In assessing the property, you'll be well served to get additional sets of eyes involved in the process. (It doesn't always take an expert to determine what they like and don't like about a property. Don't hesitate to secure the services of family and friends for this process.) As you list improvements which need to be made to the property, you should categorize those improvements as Must Make or Could Make, or whatever similar category titles work for you. It's important that you prioritize the improvements you want to make, as you may well have limited time or budget in which to make these improvements and you'll need to decide which changes can be placed on the backburner and which changes need to be done before the property is rented.

2) Make sure you have the funds available to make the changes you want to make. Hopefully you'll have done this before you purchased your property, but before you start doing any renovations, you'll need to make sure you have the funds to do so and then after you get estimates on the different projects involved in rehabbing the property, you'll then establish a budget to determine how much you are willing to spend to make the necessary changes. Again, you should already have an idea of what these changes will cost before you purchase the property. Then after you purchase the property, you can fine tune or itemize any cost estimates and determine where you'll have to cut corners in the rehabbing process.

3) Shop around. Especially for newbies, you'll have to spend some time shopping around for contractors and materials. Although no one would ever suggest that you should go with the cheapest available, especially when it comes to materials, you'll probably be very surprised at how much material costs and labor costs vary. You may be able to save thousands of dollars by doing a thorough job of shopping for both contractors and materials.

4)   Line up contractors, service providers in advance. As mentioned above, it's OK to shop around for contractors and service providers, especially with your first rental property purchase. You'll want to determine pricing and also make sure you find people that you are comfortable in working with. At the same time, it won't hurt to interview multiple contractors; in the event that you have trouble with one contractor, you could move to the second contractor on the list, if necessary. And, most importantly, don't wait until the last minute to schedule contractors such as plumbers, electricians, painters, landscapers. You should remember that these people are busy working on other projects and you can't expect them to drop everything they're doing to work on your project. A successful contractor often has a busy schedule that is filled weeks, if not months, in advance. Keep this in mind when you are putting together your rehab schedule.

5)   Draw up a realistic calendar. As you plan your rehab project, you'll need to develop a calendar which lists dates for all of the major tasks. You'll probably start by having contractors visit the property to quote costs for their project. At the same time you are showing them what needs to be done, you should ask them about their availability for the project. When can they start? When would they finish? This information will help you establish your calendar. And one word of caution for you as you set up your schedule. Try not to have too much going on at the property at the same time. If you have the plumber, the electrician, the cabinet installers, and the painter all there at the same time, they're likely to get in each other's way and you're likely to experience delays, or possibly even damages.

6) **Track expenses.** You should be tracking your expenses throughout the process to make sure you're going to make budget. Nothing worse than getting halfway through a project, only to find out that you've overspent by a lot and you going to have to delay the project until you can come up with more money. You can use an Excel spreadsheet or Quickbooks to track your expenditures throughout the project. On the plus side, you might find that you are under budget and this might allow you to add some of the bells and whistles you have previously eliminated when you originally did your budget.

7) **Be there.** With a rehab project like this, it's going to be important for someone to be there to supervise while the work is going on. If you don't have the time to do that, you should hire or enlist the services of someone that can do that for you. We've heard stories of contractors that have ripped up floors in the wrong rooms, installed cabinets in the wrong rooms, removed the tiles from the wrong bathroom, etc. Yes, we even had a roofer whose people tore off half the shingles from the neighbor's house by mistake. These things happen and they happen often. So, it will behoove you to have someone there to supervise or answer questions while the work is going on.

8) **Have a Plan B.** What happens if one of your contractors gets delayed on another project? What happens if there is a torrential downpour when your landscaper is supposed to plant the new shrubs or the exterior painter is supposed to paint the outside of the house? What happens if one of your contractors is a total bust and you have to secure another contractor to do the job they were supposed to do? Although you can never plan for these possible hiccups, you should know that these things can and will happen. And when they do, you will have to be flexible and you'll have to move to Plan B, sometimes in urgency. (If you don't have a Plan B, you're going to have to come up with one.) This is never an easy or fun part of the process, but how

you handle it may well determine if you're going to be good at being a rental real estate property owner. Most successful rental property owners are problem solvers, and many take pride in their ability to adapt as problems arise.

9) Secure your materials. Keep your materials in a safe and secure place. Keep them out of the workers' way, so they're not impacting the way the work is being done or they are not a danger to the workers. Keep the materials in a secure place so they won't get damaged by rain or snow or so they won't get stolen.

10) Determine a sequence. As you set up a schedule for the rehabbing projects in your new rental property, it's going to be important for you to determine a practical sequence in which projects should be done and materials should be installed. A lot of this is just simple common sense. For example, don't install the new carpeting until the walls are painted, the new appliances are installed, and the laborers are done tracking through the house. Don't install new kitchen or bathroom cabinets until the painting in those rooms has been completed. Have the electricians and plumbers provide their services early in the process, unless there is a reason they should do later.

The Most Important Rehabs for All Rental Properties

In rehabbing your rental property that are a few items that should absolutely be inspected before you lease to a tenant. Some of the items are frequently overlooked; others can have a major impact on your relationship with the tenant and a major impact on your investment.

1) The Roof. We've seen instances of people who have purchased rental properties without even inspecting the roof. That's a big mistake. The roof is an essential structural component of any building and you should make sure you have it inspected, ideally before you purchase the property. If you have to add a new roof to your rental property, that's not going to be a petty cash expenditure. You should know the condition of your roof, so you can plan accordingly for any repairs that need to be done. A faulty roof cannot be ignored and you'll be risking the value of your investment if you don't make sure the roof remains in good condition.

2) **Carpeting, Painting.** Common, relatively inexpensive things that are normally included in any rehab project. If you have shabby carpeting or painting, it's likely to impact your ability to lease the property, as it's one of the first things that prospective tenants see.

3) **Windows.** Like roofs, not an inexpensive proposition. From an investment standpoint, you'll want to make sure your property has upgraded windows as it enhances the value of your property. Also, from a tenant standpoint, a good set of windows can help substantially with the insulation of the house and will reduce heating and air conditioning bills.

4) **Electrical.** 200 amp panels recommended, as they are not much more expensive than 100 amp panels.

5) **Heating/Air Conditioning/Vents.** It's a good idea to have these inspected at least once a year, even when the property is occupied. Heating and air conditioning systems are not cheap and you'll want to make sure they are kept in good condition. You can't expect that your tenants will do so. We've heard stories of properties that have had fires because dryer vents were clogged. Routine maintenance can easily prevent major problems.

6) **Furnace.** Along the same lines, you need to keep tabs on the furnace in your property. An average furnace will last 10-15 years and, as you might expect, they are somewhat expensive. You'll be well served if you know what condition your furnace is in and when you might need another, so you can plan accordingly. You'll also want to make sure that you or your tenant is changing filters in your furnace regularly, as clogged furnace filters can do some serious damage.

7) **Sewer system/plumbing.** Make sure you monitor the sewer system in your property. A sewer backup can cause some serious damage to the property. You should certainly have the sewer lines inspected and checked at the outset of any rehab project. And then have them checked regularly, depending on how likely they are to get clogged. For example, someone who owns a home with a lot of trees on the property may find that they have tree roots that clog the sewer pipes regularly. If you know this, you can schedule routine maintenance on a regular basis to prevent any major problems. At the same time you're checking the sewer system, it's probably a good idea to check all the drains and the garbage disposal. If you can make sure these things are clear before your tenant moves in, you may be able to eliminate middle-of-the-night calls informing you of these problems.

8) **Water heaters.** Water heaters are fairly inexpensive. They'll normally last 8 to 12 years, depending on how hard the water is in your area and how good the water heater is. If your water heater is approaching this age, it's probably a good idea to start thinking about a new one.

Home Improvements to Instantly Boost the Value of Your Property

In the previous section, we focused on functional and structural items which are strongly recommended for any rental rehab project. Now let's take a look at some of the "funner" stuff, things you can do to enhance the cosmetic value, the eye appeal, and the ultimate value of your property. You'll note that many of these cosmetic enhancements are not major renovation or expensive projects. With many of these recommendations, you'll find that you can boost the value or appeal of your property without breaking the bank.

1)   Bathroom facelift.   Regardless of how small it is, the bathroom is considered one of the focal points of any home. Bathroom upgrades including re-tiling, re-caulking, replacing or re-glazing tubs or showers, or a new vanity with modern lighting are all things you can do to upgrade your bathrooms. Research shows that bathroom upgrades can add more to the value of a residential property than any other room. The payback on bathroom upgrades is more than double the amount invested in the upgrade.

2)   Landscape redesign.   Another eye appeal project which can add substantial and immediate value to a property. Things such as trimming shrubs and trees, weeding, and adding new plants or bushes can easily add to the value and the curb appeal of a property.

3)   Minor kitchen remodel.   You don't have to spend a fortune to increase the eye appeal of your kitchen. Simple things such as updated appliances, new counter tops, and new cabinet facings can easily increase the appeal of your kitchen. New floor tiles and new wallpaper are also things that can be done inexpensively to enhance your kitchen.

4)   Exterior improvements.   Besides some landscaping enhancements, you can increase the curb appeal of your home with a new paint job, new siding, new trim, or a new front door.

5) **Bedroom conversion.** Is there a marginal, non-essential room in the house that you can convert to another bedroom? Even if it is a small bedroom, that extra bedroom can add substantially to the value of a home.

All of the above-mentioned renovations can add substantially to the eye appeal of your home, making it easier to rent. As most homes are now viewed online before a potential renter even inquires about them, eye appeal/curb appeal is more important than ever. If you don't have an attractive property, it's going to be difficult to even get potential renters to visit your property. And from a long-term standpoint, these cosmetic enhancements can also add financial value to your home many times over. For each of the five renovations listed above, the lowest expected payback on the investment is in the 90th percentile. This means that with whatever you invest in any of these areas, you should be able to almost double your investment as it adds to the value of your property.

Chapter 7—Managing Your Rental

OK, you're done rehabbing your rental property. Now it's time to rent the property. Some property owners make the mistake of thinking that most of their work is done and most of their problems are over once they've finished preparing their property for rental. That might well be a drastic misassumption. If you aren't renting to the right people, your problems might just be starting and you might be jeopardizing all of the time and money you've already spent on the property. Getting good tenants into your properties is extremely important. Once the property is ready, your ability to get good tenants may well be the key to whether your property is profitable or not. With this in mind, we have some solid recommendations on what you can do to minimize tenant problems.

Finding Great Tenants for Your Rental

1) **Don't discriminate.** Before we get into the basics of what you should do to find great tenants, we should caution you not to discriminate. There are federal laws that prohibit discrimination and you'll need to adhere to these regulations when renting your property. We've read numerous stories of landlords who have been sued for their discriminatory practices and you won't want to be one of those people. Settlement amounts for these lawsuits are sometimes more that the value of the property itself, so we certainly implore you not to discriminate in renting your properties.

The Fair Housing Act prohibits discrimination in the following areas:

--Race or color

--Religion

--National origin

--Sex

--Familial status. (You can't discriminate against families with kids.)

--Disability

2) Create a detailed rental application. Leasing a property is serious business and you should not hesitate to use a detailed rental application that will help you gather the information you'll need to determine whether to rent to the applicant or not. Included in the application should be the following items:

a) Personal references. Ask for two or three personal references, preferably non-family references. Then you need to make sure that you follow up with these references before you rent to the applicant. When you are talking to these references, we suggest that one of the questions you ask them if the tenant has told them why they are moving and then make sure that matches what he is telling you.

b) Employment history. This information might tell you something as to how stable the applicant is. If they've done a lot of job switching or there are an unusual number of employment gaps, this might be an indicator that they won't be a stable tenant. And with employment history, you'll probably be well served to check that the history listed on the application is correct. It's not all that unusual for people to fabricate information on rental applications.

c) Previous rental history. It's possible that your applicant won't have any rental history. (i.e.—recent high school or college grad, retired couple who have downsized, etc.) However, if a history is listed, you'll do well to contact the previous landlords. Instead of just confirming residency, you should also ask other questions that might help you in determining whether the applicant will be a good tenant. Those questions might include: Did they pay their rent on time? Were they clean? Respectful to neighbors and staff? Did they leave the unit in good condition when they vacated? Did they give the required notice before moving out? Did any of the neighbors complain about them? Did they require an unusual amount of attention as a tenant? Would you lease to them again?

d) Credit checks. Run a credit check on your prospective tenant and take it seriously. Some landlords set a credit score limit in renting to tenants. A required credit score of 650 is a common requirement. If the candidate seems like a decent candidate, but the credit score isn't what you'd like it to be, you might ask if there is an explanation for the low score. Credit checks will also tell you how much debt the applicant has (see income-to-debt ratio note in the following verify income category), whether he or she has been evicted from a previous property, and whether he or she has any judgments against them.

e) Verify income. It's not unusual for rental applicants to fudge on their stated income, so it will behoove you to take the time to verify their income. Contact their current employer and verify income, length of employment, standing with the company, and attendance record. As a rule of thumb, you'll want to find a tenant whose monthly income is three times the proposed rent amount. There are exceptions to this, of course, such as retired couples who may have limited income, but have nest eggs that can easily accommodate the rent amounts.

When we say that ideally a tenant should have income which is three times his rent amount, we should also harken back to the credit check/credit score, where you should make a note to check the applicant's income-to-debt ratio. For example, you might have one applicant who has an income of $3000 a month; another who has an income of $2500 a month. You might think that the higher-earning candidate is always the better candidate, but that's not always the case.

Maybe the higher-earning candidate has debt payments totaling $1500 a month, while the lower-earning candidate has no debts at all, except for a nominal car payment. In this instance, the lower-earning candidate might be a better candidate, at least from a financial standpoint.

f) Criminal background check. Criminal history is one of the most "lied about" things on job and rental applications. So, we highly recommend that you do a criminal background check on any prospective tenant that you're interested in. Doing a criminal background check yourself can be very time-consuming, so you may want to use a tenant screening company to do this for you.

Use the information you collect to evaluate the tenant realistically. You should obviously have more concerns about a tenant who has had drug-dealing or sexual assault charges than someone who has multiple speeding tickets. Also, pay attention to when the crimes were committed. Is it a 50-year old man who had some drunk driving charges in his 20s and hasn't had anything since? Or has he had more recent offenses? This information may well make a difference as to whether your prospective tenant is a good candidate or not.

A couple of other quick notes about criminal background checks: If you hire a tenant screening company to provide a background check for you, most of these companies will do a federal and statewide record search, a county search, a Department of Corrections search, and a sexual offender database search. Although this is public information, it can be difficult and time-consuming to gather if you haven't done it before; the cost to use a tenant screening company is nominal. (There is no nationwide criminal database, so criminal background checks are not as thorough or as simple as you might thing they would be.) Also, we should mention that some states, including California, prohibit landlords from discriminating against prospective tenants who have committed certain types of crimes. This means that you'll want to become familiar with whatever your local laws are before you rule out a tenant due to criminal history. That being said, certain past criminal history, including domestic assault, drug- or human-trafficking, drug-dealing, etc., are all activities that should raise immediate red flags for landlords.

g) Face-to-face; gut instinct. When you show your property to your prospective tenants, you should make an effort to get to know them. Hopefully, you can use your meeting with them to start to establish a relationship and maybe get a gut feel as to whether they will be a good tenant or not. And don't hesitate to ask them questions which might help you in determining whether they are a good candidate. Any questions should obviously be appropriate and not too personal (you're not conducting an interrogation), but you might be able to secure some information which will be helpful in evaluating the candidate. Here are some questions you might ask an applicant: Why are you looking to move? Where do you live now? Have you ever rented before? Have you ever had a problem with a landlord before? If you are accepted to rent the property, do you have any idea as to how long you might rent it? What do you do for a living? Do you smoke or have pets? Do you think you'll be a good tenant?

You'll note that some of these questions will be the same questions that are asked on your application form. That's OK. You may be surprised to find out that sometimes the answers you get on an application form don't jibe with the answers to the same questions in a face-to-face meeting. If so, that might indicate some red flags.

Also, in starting to establish a relationship with a possible tenant, you'll then find it easier to go back to them if any questions should arise from their credit check, their reference check, their background check, etc. You might be able to determine how forthcoming they will be, for example, if you ask them why their credit score is "iffy". Maybe there is a logical explanation for their credit score. If everything seems to fit, except maybe one thing, don't hesitate to ask the applicant for an explanation...unless you have many other legitimate applicants for the same property. Either way, the bottom line is that you should use your face-to-face interaction with the prospective tenant to get a feel as to whether they'll be a good tenant. Gut instinct won't trump some of the facts you secure regarding your applicant, however it does count for something and it might be the difference-maker in choosing one candidate over another.

And before we leave this topic, we should mention how important it is to keep good tenants once you have them. You can do this by responding promptly to any tenant requests or questions and also by establishing an open line of communication with them. Let them know that you are there to help them with their needs and it won't hurt to ask them occasionally if they are satisfied with the rental or if they have any feedback regarding the property. If you don't know it already, you'll find out soon...good tenants can make your life a whole lot easier and they can make the difference between a profitable property and an unprofitable property.

We encourage to treat your tenants just as if you would treat a valued customer in any other business. We know successful landlords who send birthday cards, holiday cards, and thank you cards to tenants. We also know landlords who have "exit interviews" with tenants who are vacating the property. In doing so, they'll look for feedback regarding the property. The feedback provided may be helpful to the landlord in future endeavors. Either way, you should always remember that the better the relationship you can develop with your tenant, the more likely it will be for them to continue to rent from you. As you're well aware, any time you have to turn over a lease, you're going to have to spend time to find a new tenant and you also make have some vacancy time in which the property is draining your bank account instead of adding to it.

Strategies for Managing Rental Property

It probably won't surprise you when we point out that if you don't manage a property correctly, that property can turn into a nightmare for you. Instead of being the profit center you hope it to be, it can become a giant money pit and leave you wondering why you ever decided to get into rental real estate. Thankfully, there are a number of different ways you can manage a property successfully. Some rental property owners will be successful with a strictly hands-on approach. Other owners will be successful by outsourcing everything. And others will be successful with a mix of hands-on and outsourcing.

Before you get into these different strategies, it's important to explain the three different areas of managing a property. You'll need to focus on these three areas if you want to achieve maximum profit potential with your rental properties.

1) **Manage tenants.** As a rental property owner, you or whoever you hire to do so is going to be responsible for managing tenants. The task of managing tenants includes leasing the property (and determining the viability of tenants), collecting rent, and developing/implementing/updating lease agreements. It also involves handling tenant requests (repair requests and information requests) promptly, coordinating move in and move out dates, and, unfortunately, sometimes evictions.

2) **Managing the property for maintenance and inspections.** As a landlord you'll also be responsible for the maintenance and the upkeep of the property. With commercial property or multi-unit properties, this may include the responsibilities of arranging for

common area maintenance (grass cutting and landscaping, janitorial services (including restrooms), garbage collection, snow removal, heat and running water, roof leaks, etc. Obviously, residential properties will include less responsibility. In some residential renter agreements, tenants may be responsible for their own snow shoveling, lawn mowing, garbage collection, etc. Unfortunately, with maintenance, you usually won't be able to plan in advance. Problems are likely to spring up at the most unlikely of times, and you'll have to make sure that you or whoever you hire to handle these tasks will be available at "the drop of a dime". Also, you should know that you will have to arrange to accommodate inspections of your property. Local inspectors may want to inspect your property to make sure it meets all health and safety codes, including fire codes. Mortgage and insurance companies may want to inspect the property to make sure that the property corresponds with the amounts they are lending or for which they are insuring.

3) **Managing finances.** As a rental property owner, it's going to be important for you to keep a constant handle on how much money is coming in and how much is going out. As we've said before, being a rental property owner is not a hobby, and you'll want to make sure that your properties are as profitable as possible. Rental property financial responsibilities include collecting rent from tenants and then making payments to the various parties involved, including mortgage payments, insurance, and taxes. It also may include making utility payments and paying any fees and fines.

As a landlord, you're going to have to pay attention to all three of these areas. Although it is natural for a person to drift toward the tasks they enjoy doing and wander away from those tasks they don't enjoy, you are going to have to make sure that you are not ignoring any of these areas of responsibility. If you do neglect any of these areas, you're likely to pay the consequences and your neglect will most certainly impact the profitability of your property. That being said, some landlords will make it a point to outsource any of the responsibilities they have no interest in doing, as they are aware that they will tend to neglect these areas. Now that we've outlined the different responsibilities of owning a property, it's time to look at three different strategies to use in managing properties.

The Hands-on/Do-it-Yourself Strategy. If you intend to be a hands-on/do-it-yourself landlord, you're going to have to be a person of many different hats. Landlords will opt for the hands-on strategy for a number of reasons, including total control, the ability to keep costs at a minimum, and the ability to identify and solve problems immediately. This is a lot easier for single unit or owner-occupied properties; it's a lot more difficult for commercial or larger multi-unit properties.

The downside of a hands-on management approach is that you may be attempting to do some things that you're really not knowledgeable enough to do. For example, a rental property owner who sets out to do everything involved may have to be an accounting expert, a legal expert, a maintenance expert (roofer, electrician, plumber). It's likely that you are still going to have to outsource some of the responsibilities involved in being a rental property owner, and you shouldn't feel bad about that. It's normal. In being a hands-on owner, you're likely going to have to be available 24/7/365, and, as mentioned above, you're not going to be able to control when problems arise. Some people find this overwhelming and that's why many owners end up outsourcing certain tasks and responsibilities. Other owners soon find that their time can be more valuably spent doing other things and they'll then outsource certain tasks. As an example, maybe you decide to draft your own lease agreement without the assistance or expertise of a real estate attorney. You could in fact find examples on the internet and then draft your own agreement. But you'll also have to make sure you are familiar with local leasing laws and regulations, which are different in individual states. By the time you finish researching rental agreements, you may find out that you would have been better off hiring a real estate attorney. Or maybe you miss one of the local laws in your agreement and find out later that this omission has left an expensive loophole in your agreement. Bottom line is that you'll have to decide which tasks you're capable of performing and which tasks you're willing to take the time to perform. In some instances, you'll decide that you'll want to outsource some of these responsibilities.

As you can see from the above description, a hands-on management approach is mostly suited toward a landlord who either owns a small number of properties, who has a lot of experience managing properties, or who wants total control in managing those properties.

The Mixed Responsibility Strategy. Most landlords, even those on the smaller spectrum, tend to use a mixed responsibility strategy in managing their properties. We touched on some of this above when we described the possible cons of trying to do everything yourself. Are you a legal expert? An accounting expert? A plumber? An electrician? A roofer? What if you get caught up in an expensive legal battle because you tried to draft your own rental agreement and were not aware of important local rules and regulations? What if you miss a key loophole in paying your taxes because you tried to do your own accounting instead of hiring an accounting expert? You get the picture…sometimes we can get into trouble by trying to be all things to all people. We'll be better served to outsource responsibilities that are outside our areas of expertise or interest.

The biggest benefits of using a mixed responsibility strategy are that you'll free up some of your time and you'll also be assured that your protecting your physical and financial assets by using experts. On the negative side, you'll lose some control and you will be relying on others, placing your reputation as a landlord in the hands of others. So, if you are building your rental portfolio, and you're past the stage of owning your first rental property, the mixed responsibility strategy is probably best for you. The average landlord handles some responsibilities himself and farms out other responsibilities to others.

Outsource Management Completely. There are a number of reasons why rental property owners will opt to outsource all management responsibilities. Some owners will do so because they own non-local properties and it's simply not logistically feasible for them to be hands-on property owners. Some owners own so many properties that they can't be involved on a hands-on basis. And finally, some investors have real estate investments as just a part of their total investments and they simply don't have the time to be hands-on managers.

Most of the landlords who outsource management responsibilities will either hire managers for their properties or they will utilize a management company. Managers or management companies should be able to perform or arrange for all of the tasks that are involved in managing the property: securing and screening tenants, arranging for repairs, coordinating move ins and move outs, collecting rents, pursuing delayed rents, evictions, coordinating routine maintenance and long-term maintenance and upgrades. A good manager or management company should obviously have a good working relationship with the owner of the property. It's obvious that mismanagement of any property could result in the demise of that property.

The upside of hiring a manager or a management company for your properties will be that you will free up a lot of your time. You won't be the one getting the phone calls in the middle of the night from tenants telling you their heat isn't working. And, if you do your due diligence in hiring a good manager or a good management company, you'll know that you'll be using experts in managing these properties instead of trying to wear hats that don't fit you.

The downsides of outsourcing everything involve costs and control. Especially if you are a small-time rental property owner, you're going to have to be aware that a manager, management company, or any of the companies you hire to assist with the responsibilities of owning a rental property (attorneys, accountants, plumbers, electricians) are going to cost money. And, the money you pay them will have an influence on your profitability. That being said, not hiring good managers or other experts in their field, may impact your property's ability to be successful in the long term.

12 Must-Know Tips from Rental Property Experts

Although we've included plenty of tips throughout this book on how to manage your rental properties, we have some additional tips to offer or to expand upon:

1) Use professional photographs to market your property. You can't derive any rental income from your property if you can't rent it. The importance of good photographs is often underestimated in marketing a property. It's no secret that most prospective tenants will want to view the property and the unit before deciding whether they will visit the property. In order not to get ruled out immediately, you'll want to make sure that you are using attractive photos that properly highlight the property. In advertising your property online, show as many photos as possible. Show each room in the property and also the exterior of the property. If the property has any unique features, show closeup photos of those features. On the other hand, try not to highlight outdated features. Do whatever is possible to show a clean and uncluttered property. Remember that when prospective tenants view your property online, they'll likely be comparing against photos of other properties. Some property owners hire professional photographers to use in marketing their properties. In advertising your rental property, you'll want to make sure it stands out from other properties in the same rental category.

2)   **Consider allowing pets.** We've all heard horror stories about how a pet can demolish a residence. But then again, some people demolish their residences also. As homeownership is dwindling, you should know that an open pet policy, usually for dogs and cats, might increase the marketability of your property. You can restrict pet occupancy as you see fit (by limiting the number of pets or the size of pets), and you can even seek an additional deposit or an additional rental fee for a pet. Obviously, when you say you allow cats in the unit, you won't want the tenant to have tigers or lions in there. Ha. And many property owners will restrict dog size to medium or small. Great Danes not allowed! If you're having difficulty marketing and renting your property, this might be an option to consider. We know a rental property owner who rents to a lot of baby boomers who have previously owned homes and are downsizing. He does well in allowing pets in his properties, making them available to a lot more prospective tenants.

3)   **Install smart locks in your rentals.** If you're not familiar with smart locks, they are electronic devices which allow keyless entry into a property through use of a smartphone. Although there is obviously a cost involved in installing keyless entry, research shows that these costs typically pay for themselves within seven months of the expenditure. As competitive as the rental market can be, time is money when it comes to leasing properties. When a tenant asks you to show a property and you're not able to accommodate them immediately because of schedule conflicts, they may move on to the next property and you may lose that prospective tenant. Or if you are delayed in showing them the property, it's likely that the lease may be delayed. Studies show that properties with smart locks lease 3-7 days faster than properties with traditional locks. Smart locks are not only

safer and more convenient for tenants, they also add to the value of the property and they enable self-showings in which the landlord or the manager don't have to be present.

4)   Landscaping/simple updating. Curb appeal/eye appeal are extremely important. There are many inexpensive ways you can make your property more attractive to prospective tenants. Upon visiting your property, any prospective tenant will see the exterior of your home before they see the interior. If they are already "turned off" before they see the inside of the place, you may have already lost your chance to rent the property. Many landscaping changes can be done on a modest budget. These changes will not just increase the marketability of the property, they will also increase the overall value of the property. Same goes for any features in your property that are noticeably outdated. Features such a granite kitchen counter tops, stainless steel kitchen sinks, well-lit bathrooms, and updated appliances can easily increase the marketability of the property without costing you a fortune.

5)   Rental walk-through. Once you have rented the property, it will behoove you are your property manager to do an immediate walk-through with the new tenant. This walk-through will allow you to identify any immediate concerns that the tenant has. It will also allow you to document any possible concerns. It's better to identify these concerns at the outset of the lease, so any required changes can be addressed immediately. Also, it is better to pinpoint any problems at the beginning of the lease instead of at the end. For example, if you missed some carpet stains at the outset of the lease (maybe the guy installing the new water heater had some leakage when he removed the old water heater), those stains should be documented and photographed on the walk-through, so this will not be a point of contention at the end of the lease when the deposit refund comes into question. These things should always be documented, because by the time you hit the end of the lease, you may well have forgotten about these problems until the tenant brings them up again.

6) **Upgrading when the property is vacant.** Whenever possible, you should do your upgrading between leases or whenever the property is vacant. Obviously, you won't want to inconvenience your current tenants with upgrades, if those upgrades can wait and are not emergency upgrades. And we should also mention that it is important for you to take the time to reevaluate your property between every tenant and, if the unit needs upgrading or renovation, then you may be able to delay the start date of the new lease while you make the renovations.

7) **Attend to tenant concerns immediately.** We mentioned this briefly before, but it's going to be important for you as a landlord to always address tenant concerns and requests immediately. If a tenant thinks that you are lackadaisical concerning their requests, they may get the feeling that you don't care and you're only interested in taking their money at the end of each month. If the tenant requests a repair and you can't get someone there to rectify the problem immediately, keep your client posted on exactly when they might expect the problem to be fixed. Again, a reminder, tenants who feel that a landlord is attentive to their needs are much more likely to extend their leases.

8) **Express appreciation.** A landlord/tenant relationship should be a two-way street and you should make a point to tell your tenants how much you appreciate them (if, in fact, you do). Some landlords send birthday cards, holiday cards, or thank you cards to tenants. Other landlords will send handwritten notes telling the appropriate tenants how much they always appreciate their prompt rental payments or how they appreciate how they always keep the property clean and in good condition. Again, a tenant who feels appreciated is more likely to extend the lease.

9) **Require renter's insurance.** This is something that often gets overlooked by landlords. You'll do well to require your renter to have renter's insurance and to demand proof of that insurance. You might think that a tenant is the only one who can benefit from his own insurance. Well, you can also benefit. Let's say that the tenant leaves the bathtub faucet running and floods the unit...or they leave the stove on while they are taking a phone call and a fire results. Or, what happens if your tenant totally trashes the unit, far exceeding the security deposit you have for that unit? In these instances, you will be able to benefit from your tenant's insurance.

10) **Keep security deposits separate.** Speaking of security deposits, please remember that when a tenant makes a security deposit, that's not your money and you will be wise to keep that money separate and in escrow. If you are ever unable to refund the security deposit at the end of the lease, you are likely to be subject to penalties and fines which well exceed the security deposit amounts.

11) **Use property management software.** One lost receipt can cost you a possible tax deduction. A lost or misplaced lease can cost you months in eviction court proceedings. Technology can help you manage your property. Instead of having misplaced notes or paperwork in multiple areas of your office, you can have it all in one place. You can use technology to keep track of your property listing, to keep track of rental payments and repair requests and history, signed leases, and tenant screenings. It's good to have all this information in the same place. A property management software program can help you do that.

12) **Be willing to make concessions and extend lease terms to good tenants.** As mentioned before, finding good tenants can be a trying and difficult task. So, once you find a good tenant, you'll want to work

hard to keep them. A vacant property is going to cost you money, even if it is only vacant a month. Along the same lines, you'll have to spend additional time in securing a new tenant, who may not be a good tenant like the last one was.

We've previously mentioned the importance of promptly addressing tenant requests and also establishing a good line of communication with your tenants. Another way to keep good tenants is to offer to extend them or to make concessions if they extend their lease. We've known landlords who have had a lot of success in making or offering renewal concessions. Examples of concessions might be a free month's rent with minimum extension of 12 months or more, no rental increase if lease is extended by a specified date, or, if you live in a northern area and a lease is due to expire during the winter season, you might offer to extend the lease at the same rate for just a few months. This will allow your tenant to vacate at a time when the weather is more conducive to a move and it will allow you as the landlord a better time to find a new tenant, when the rental market is more active. Again, open lines of communication with a tenant can make your job as a landlord a lot easier. Keep in touch with your tenant to find out what their intentions are when the lease expires. This will help you from a planning standpoint and it may also help you get a feel for whether your tenant is even open to an extension.

In a similar vein, if rental rates in your market have been decreasing, and your lease rate is now above market rate, offering a free month's rent or even half a month's rent for an extension might increase your chances for an extension and keep your tenant from shopping other properties.

Chapter 8—Precautions

If you're thinking of getting into the real estate rental business, you've most likely heard some tremendous success stories along the way. Those stories may have amplified your interest in the business. That being said, you need to also be aware of the possible pitfalls of the business. Human nature tells us that investors are not as quick to tell horror stories as they are to tell success stories. Any business that has tremendous success also probably has some serious risks. This is the case with the real estate rental business. We would never attempt to put a damper on your interest to enter the industry, but we want to remind you to go into the real estate rental business with your eyes wide open, just as you would within any other business. Here are some common reasons why rental property investors fail:

1) **Underestimating overall startup capital.** Some investors make the mistake of underestimating what their startup costs will be for a rental property. They'll look at the sell price of the property itself, and then they'll underestimate the costs to renovate that property or the cost to make it marketable. Please know that although the sell price of the property may be the main expense, you'll have to have enough money to make the property marketable. You'll be well served to do the research on renovation costs before you purchase the property. You'll also do well to pad the amounts you estimate, so you have an extra cushion in there for projects you may have overlooked or cost estimates that come in higher than originally quoted.

We always caution rental property investors not to think that their spending stops with the closing on the property. For some property owners, that's when the spending starts. Even if the property you purchase is in good condition, you may have to do some updates to bring your property up to code, especially if you are going from what was an owner-occupied property to a rental property. Many states and municipalities have different regulations for rental properties and you'll be well-served to know what the rules are in your state and municipality. If you don't, you could be in for some expensive surprises.

2) **Underestimating or not planning for unexpected/emergency repairs.** This is another pitfall that can lead to failure. The furnace you thought had three to five more years in it goes out and you receive a late-night call on a cold evening from your tenant telling you that he now has no heat. You have to contact and hire a heating company immediately to find out what the problem is. The technician you hire tells you that your furnace is shot and you'll have to get a new one. New furnaces are not cheap and you'll have to have access to immediate cash for the new furnace and installation. Either that, or you could face legal action from a disgruntled tenant. You get the picture. If you're going to get involved in the rental property business, you're going to have to have contingency funds or funding to cover unexpected and sometimes substantial emergencies.

3) **Deadbeat Tenants/Problem Tenants.** OK, you've purchased your first rental property and spent two months rehabbing it and another month securing a tenant for the property. The monthly rent arrives on time each of the first three months, but then you don't receive the rent for the fourth month. You've had a difficult time reaching the tenant and when you finally reach him, he informs you that they've had some family emergencies and he's been unable to come up with the funds for this month's rent. He'll try to get you some money soon, but things aren't looking promising as he was laid off from his job soon after they moved into the rental. Well, you certainly didn't expect that.

Now, you'll quickly have to become familiar with the eviction process. Not only will you be missing the income you expected from the rental, you now might have to hire an attorney to evict the tenant. And how long before you can evict the tenant? States have different laws regarding tenant eviction and some of those laws allow tenants to stay well past their welcome. And then you'll have to spend time marketing and leasing the property again. It might take you 30-60 days past the eviction to lease the property again. You get the picture. You'll need to have contingency funds to account for deadbeat tenants. Yes, you can reduce the chances of a deadbeat tenant by vetting that tenant properly before you lease them the property, but even with that, life happens and you may be presented with tenants who are no longer able to pay their rent.

We heard an interesting story from a first-time rental property investor who decided to rent out his condo after he purchased a new home. He rented his condo to a man and his girlfriend. The tenant was a well-paid attorney at a reputable law firm. The girlfriend, who was not on the lease, had a fledgling modeling career. Rent payments from this tenant were always prompt until they stopped completely five months into the lease. In contacting the tenant, the landlord was told that the man and his girlfriend had had a blowout and the man was now living with a friend of his instead of living in the rental unit. The girlfriend, now apparently the ex-girlfriend, had continued to live in the rental unit after the fight.

The tenant, an attorney, stated that he no longer intended to make payments (even though he had a solid 12-month lease, and he would not be living there. If his ex-girlfriend wanted to pick up the lease, that would be fine with him. Left to fend for himself against a tenant who was an attorney, the landlord knew he was in the middle of a fiasco. He did a surprise inspection on the property and found out that the front door of the condo had extensive damage, probably from someone who attempted to break down a door in a domestic fight. Upon entering the unit, he also found that there were cats in the unit despite that fact that pets were not allowed in the lease agreement. He also noted substantial carpet damage from what looked to be hair dye.

Who woulda thunk it? The landlord had vetted his tenant properly, he had rented to a party who could easily pay the monthly rent and someone who seemed likely to be a tenant who would care for the property. Yet, now here he was, having to file legal proceedings against his attorney tenant. When the landlord contacted the girlfriend, he found that she was between modeling gigs and couldn't pay the entire amount of the rent because her ex was refusing to help her. She offered to pay half the amount of the rent. This was unacceptable to the landlord and he knew that he'd have to hire an attorney to initiate legal proceedings against his tenant. Thankfully, the woman agreed to move out at the end of the month, so he wouldn't have to evict her.

Yes, it's a horror story, but it does have a "happy" ending. Just before the landlord was about to initiate illegal proceedings against his deadbeat attorney tenant, he mentioned the problem to his racquetball buddy, a corporate attorney for the company the landlord worked for. Ironically, the corporate attorney had a close working relationship with the law firm that the deadbeat tenant worked for. The corporate attorney called a partner at the law firm the deadbeat worked for. The same day, the deadbeat attorney delivered a check for the past due amount and all the remaining months on the lease. The landlord later found out that the partner at the law firm of the deadbeat had read the riot act to the deadbeat and told him that if he ever expected to make partner someday, he'd be well-advised not to tarnish the sterling reputation of the law firm. With that said, the deadbeat delivered a large check covering the remaining months of the lease and he also offered to pay for the damaged door and carpeting. Bottom line, this first-time landlord got lucky. It was pure happenstance that his problem was solved as easily as it was. In most instances, the landlord would have been left "holding the bag", never seeing the remaining months owed on the lease.

This story illustrates two possible areas which can cause tenants to fail: tenant non-payment and property damage. Most of you have heard nightmarish stories about rental units which have been left in disarray by tenants. A moneycrashers.com blog told the story of a landlord who rented to a trio of college students. Again, upon non-payment, the landlord did an inspection of the property. He found a large hole in the ceiling separating the second floor from the ground floor. A large fireman's pole had been haphazardly installed to allow the tenants quick access from the upper floor to the bottom floor. The graffiti which now filled the walls of the until was the least of the landlord's concerns.

4) **Evictions.** If you're under the impression that evictions are simple, you've got another thing coming. Evictions can be expensive and time consuming. First, you may find out that the courts are backed up and you may have to wait a while for a court date. Presuming that you win the case and the court approves the eviction notice, you might then have to wait a while for the sheriff or a member of law enforcement to accompany you when you execute the eviction. You may then find that belongings have been left behind. Most state laws will not allow you to discard those belongings for a certain amount of time and you may have to pay to store them. Besides that, it shouldn't surprise anyone that vacated properties are not always left in the best of condition and you may well have to spend a lot of time and effort cleaning the unit or making damage repairs to the unit. And then there's the fact that eviction of a tenant can take up to 90 days or more in some states or municipalities that require multiple steps for eviction. So, you can see how evictions can bring down landlords. In the property rental business, time is money, and the time and money you spend in evicting a tenant can have a significant impact on your property rental business.

5)   Managing finances. Anyone who is in the rental property business can tell you that a landlord's finances don't stay constant. You can sit down at the beginning of the year and make projections for your property or properties, but you'll find that your monthly projections are seldomly going to be what you thought they would be. Things will likely be going well if your units are rented, you don't have any vacancies, your tenants are paying on time, and no major repairs are necessary. But what if you have say five units and two of them have vacancies? Are you prepared for that financially? Whether you are experiencing feast or famine with your real estate real business, you'll need to be disciplined in your finances. Even if things are going extremely well, you can't be sure when your property or properties will require major repairs or vacancies. You'll need to account for these down times by accumulating a sufficient contingency fund when times are good. In the above section on evictions, you saw how long an eviction could take. You'll want to make sure you have the funds to "ride out the storm" in the event that happens. Same goes for vacancies and difficulty in renting out a unit; same goes for major repairs. Do you have the cash on hand to replace a furnace if it goes out? These are all things to consider as a landlord.

6)   Keep your properties safe and in good condition. If you have a tenant who gets injured on your property, it's likely that you'll get sued. Even if your homeowner's insurance covers your liability, you'll probably still have to hire an attorney to represent you. Even with a homeowner's policy, you'll be expected to keep your property safe and in working order. As a landlord, it will behoove you to know what your local safety codes are and then follow those codes. We've heard stories of landlords who have been sued for large amounts because they weren't following local safety codes, either because they didn't know those codes or because they ignored those codes.

7) **Taxes.** Don't overlook property taxes. Make sure you understand the impact that property taxes can have on your property and then plan and save accordingly. It shouldn't surprise anyone to find out that property taxes can have a major impact on the bottom line of your business. By knowing these numbers in advance, you should be able to incorporate them in the rental fees to your tenants.

The above cautionary tales are certainly not meant to scare you away from buying rental properties. Buying and owning rental properties can be a very lucrative business…if done correctly. It's not all fun and games and it should never be considered a hobby. It's serious business and it's not for everyone. But if you're willing to do your homework and work diligently to become a good landlord, you'll have the opportunity to make money in the rental property business.

Good reasons to let go of rental property.

Many rental property investors wonder about when it's a good time to sell the rental property they own. There are a number of situations which are conducive toward selling your property:

1) **You can get more than you paid for it.** Your investment strategy will have an impact on whether you should sell a property that has appreciated. If the property has appreciated in value and it's bringing in profits as a rental property, you'll have to decide whether you want to sell it at any given time. Some investors will want to sell the property and cash in their chips while they can; others will prefer the monthly income they obtain from the property and will choose to hang on to the property. It should be noted that if you sell an appreciated property, you'll know exactly what you're getting for that property. If you hang on to it, you won't know if it will appreciate or depreciate in value; you also won't know if it will remain as a steady

rental profit center, depending on the area it's in and the inventory of rental properties in that area.

2) **Negative cash flow.** The late Kenny Rogers had a song that said, "You gotta know when to hold 'em, know when to fold 'em, know when to walk away, know when to run". Although those lines from his song weren't meant to describe rental properties, those lines certainly apply to rental property. If you have a property that is not making you money, it's probably time to unload it…unless you have absolute indicators that you'll be able to turn it around quickly. Some real estate investors get caught up in the idea that maybe the negative cash flow properties will change in the future or they can't let go of an emotional attachment they have to those properties. We need to remember that one of the main reasons people invest in rental property is to make money. If you have a property that is not making money, then it's probably time to fold and use the money from the sale to invest in something more profitable.

3) **A strong seller's market.** If you have a market that has a low inventory of rental properties in your area and a low mortgage rate for buyers, it's a good time to look at the possibility of selling your property. We all know that the real estate economy (and the general economy) is cyclical and you'll be well-served if you sell your property when the factors work to your advantage.

4) **The property no longer fits your plans.** Maybe you are near retirement. Maybe you have health issues. Maybe you are tired of all the attention your rental property requires. Owning rental property can be very profitable, but no one will claim that it comes without work. If the property no longer fits your plans, maybe it's time to cash in your chips.

5) **You're in a good situation with capital gains tax.** If you're not sure if you are in a good situation regarding capital gains tax, you should consult with your financial advisor. If you're able to sell your property without a lot of capital gains taxes, you're in a good position to sell.

Five Crucial Exit Strategies for Your Real Estate Investments

What's an exit strategy, you ask? Simply, it is an investment property owner's plan to remove himself or herself from an investment. Many successful real estate investors will have a specific exit plan in place when they enter into an investment. Others will wait to get into the investment and see how it is going and then develop their exit plans. Either way, it's important to develop some kind of exit plan early on in the process, so you can quickly determine when to exit the investment. Investors who don't have exit plans will often hold on to properties too long, possibly costing them thousands of dollars (sometimes ten thousands or hundred thousands of dollars).

Investors will exit properties for a number of reasons. Maybe the time is right to make a max profit on the property. Maybe they want to exit the property and use the profits to purchase higher level properties or investments. Maybe the investor has determined that real property investment just isn't for them. Maybe the investor is retiring or has health problems or a family or financial emergency.

Here are five main exit strategies for real estate investors:

1) **Fix and flip.** Although this strategy doesn't have anything to do with rental property, it deserves mention as a real estate property exit strategy because of the popularity of flipping, in which investors will purchase properties, work quickly to upgrade those properties, and then sell them for a profit.

2) **Buy and hold.** This strategy has everything to do with rental property investment, as buyers will buy property, sometimes renovate it/sometimes not, and then they will lease the property to renters with the idea of making steady cash flow from the property as they build equity. Hopefully for the investor, the property will appreciate in value at the same time it creates steady cash flow and then the buyer can sell the property at the appropriate time and turn a nice profit.

3) **Wholesaling.** This is when someone acts as a middleman in a property purchase. They will purchase the property without any intention of occupying the property or rehabbing the property, and then they will turn around and sell it for a profit to an end buyer. This exit strategy is somewhat similar to a fix and flip strategy, however the wholesaler doesn't put any sweat equity into the project (no rehabbing or renovation). Unlike flipping, which can bring huge profits if done correctly, wholesaling generally brings lower profit margins.

4) **Seller financing.** With this strategy, the seller acts as a bank. In essence, the seller finances the purchase of the property, with the seller and the buyer having a promissory note that includes the agreed-upon interest rate and a payment schedule. From a seller standpoint, the seller gets to continue to derive income from the property to cover the mortgage loan and their return on investment also increases due to the interest rate.

5) **Rent to own.** With this exit strategy, the property owner will rent the investment property to a tenant, and then after a pre-determined/set period of time, the tenant will be able to purchase the property from the seller. In some cases in a rent to own agreement, a portion of the monthly rental payment will be set aside toward the purchase of the home. This type of agreement allows the seller to

continue to derive income from the property and then if the tenant/potential buyer walks away from the property for whatever reason, the seller has still continued to establish equity in the property.

It should be pointed out that there are numerous factors that will determine whether an investor should exit a property. Long-term goals versus short-term goals will often be a factor. Purchase price of the property, value of the property, and condition of the property may also be factors. Supply and demand, profit potential, market conditions, and financing options will also be factors.

Even if an investor has an exit plan at the outset of purchasing a property, those plans can be derailed by numerous factors. If the property depreciates, the investor may want to dump sooner than expected or make wait until the property rebounds. Tenant issues might escalate or delay the sale of a property. The same goes for unexpected major maintenance costs. Poor property management can have a major impact on the profitability of a property and when that property will be sold. And finally, a distinct lack of demand can affect the exit strategy for a property. You can't sell a property for which there's no demand.

Conclusion

Well, if you've read this far, you should now know a lot more than when you started about the opportunities that are available for you in real estate property rentals. You should have a better understanding of what real estate rental investments can do for you and how you can make money from those investments. You'll know that if you can pay attention to all the areas and responsibilities of real estate rental property investment, you'll have a chance to make money, sometimes a lot of money. You'll also know that if you neglect any areas of real estate rental property investment, you'll inhibit your chances for success and possibly even fail.

You now know how to evaluate properties for possible investment and you also know how to evaluate the neighborhoods or areas those properties are in. You know all about the 1% Rule and the formula for making sure that the properties you are investing in are viable. As many of you are first-time investors, you're going to have to determine ways to finance your first property, often times without a lot of available cash. We've told you about house hacking, a great way to break into the real estate rental property business. We also given you other ideas on how to get properties with no money down and other techniques on how to save money you can use for the down payment toward your property.

We've touched briefly on commercial real estate rental property investment, which is generally for investors as they move up the food chain from novice to expert. We told you to "draft" and develop a real estate team to ensure your success as an investor and we've told you who to include on that team.

Rehabbing properties is extremely important with most Class C and some Class B rental properties. We've given you a step-by-step guide on how rehab properties. Along the same lines, you now know what kind of rehab projects are most important for rental properties. And you also know some simple and inexpensive rehab projects you can do to increase the value of the property immediately.

As a landlord, you'll have to decide how you want to manage your property. Will you want to use the hands-on approach, the mixed approach, or the outsource approach? Regardless of which approach you choose, you'll have to do everything possible to secure good tenants for your property. Good tenants can be the lifeblood of any rental property investments; bad tenants can break you.

As most people get into real estate rental to make money, you'll find that you'll be well served if you have an exit plan for the properties you invest in. "Know when to fold 'em", as Kenny Rogers would say. We've outlined the main reasons people exit properties and also the strategies they use in exiting those properties.

In conclusion, owning real estate rental property can be very lucrative financially, if you can focus on all the different areas of the business. If you can do the research to find good properties at a good price, if you can find good tenants and take care of those tenants, if you can manage the properties well, you'll have a great chance to be successful. That being said, owner rental property in not a hobby. It's not easy money; you'll have to pay attention to detail if you're going to succeed. But if you'll utilize many of the tips and techniques offered in this book, you're likely to be successful and well on the way to financial freedom.

With that said, we'll leave you with six words: Wishing you success! Let's get after it!

www.ingramcontent.com/pod-product-compliance
Lightning Source LLC
Chambersburg PA
CBHW021129080526
44587CB00012B/1196